Suburban Residence

Circumvent

J. E. Panton

Alpha Editions

This edition published in 2024

ISBN : 9789364738088

Design and Setting By
Alpha Editions
www.alphaedis.com
Email - info@alphaedis.com

As per information held with us this book is in Public Domain. This book is a reproduction of an important historical work. Alpha Editions uses the best technology to reproduce historical work in the same manner it was first published to preserve its original nature. Any marks or number seen are left intentionally to preserve its true form.

Contents

CHAPTER I FIRST STEPS ....- 1 -

CHAPTER II HALLS AND PASSAGES ....- 12 -

CHAPTER III KITCHEN AND
BASEMENTS ....- 25 -

CHAPTER IV DINING-ROOMS ....- 36 -

CHAPTER V PARLOURS..- 49 -

CHAPTER VI THIRD ROOMS...- 60 -

CHAPTER VII THE NURSERIES ....- 71 -

CHAPTER VIII BEDROOMS ....- 83 -

CHAPTER IX DRESSING-ROOMS
AND BATHROOMS..- 94 -

CHAPTER X THE GREAT SERVANT
QUESTION...- 104 -

CHAPTER I

FIRST STEPS

THE first step to take is undoubtedly to find your suburb; the second, to discover an adaptable house; and then the third and greatest is to circumvent the many death-traps, cold-givers and misery-makers which are included in the lease; although most certainly they are not apparent in it when it is carefully brought for you to sign.

The suburbs, take them how you will, are not Paradise and can never now be made so; yet for people with middle-sized incomes and aspirations after fresh air, they are undoubtedly most necessary evils. If one is in the least susceptible to noise or not strong, London, or any other of our great cities, is an impossible place of residence. Perhaps I should have put the 'not strong' first, for suburban noises are worse, really, than any others; and one can be amused on far less money in London than one can elsewhere. For there a garden and a carriage are not in the least essential, while some kind of 'pleasaunce' and some sort of vehicle are almost indispensable out of town, unless one wants to spend one's money on flies, and one's time in catching trains, and is content to risk the ruin of one's clothes and run up doctors' bills, should one be caught in the many storms which distinguish our delightful climate, and which always descend on unprotected folk on their way to and from the station. Moreover, if one has the smallest desire for peace, one must be a certain distance from the rail, or most undoubtedly madness will ensue. I have often noticed delusive advertisements of suburban paradises where nearness to the rail is held out as an inducement to the would-be tenant, and I have often longed to 'go for' the advertiser and tell him to what a fearful end he might lead some confiding young couple, for I am perfectly sure that no one who has not tried it can have the smallest idea of what nearness to the train means—at anyrate, if one selects a suburb on one of the main lines. I know, alas! for had I not four long and maddening years in a house which was about as close to the rail as it well could be without forming part and parcel of the same? I must own, when I went into the house and, looking out of the first window I came to, beheld the demon, I at once fled from the place, and flatly refused even to look at another room, and oh! how wise I should have been had I held to my own determination. But, in those days, houses were scarce. We were obliged to be in that special locality. Everyone said one got accustomed to the trains in a week, and never heard them at all after the first night or two. The garden was charming. The last tenant had lived there for years and years, and had not left it for a lunatic asylum, and so I allowed my own judgment to give way before a storm of talk and unsought advice, and entered upon a period of misery which has shortened my days and made it impossible for me to look upon that house save as a misery-maker of the first water. For indeed, far from becoming accustomed to trains, the more one lives near them the more one hears them. I used to find I regularly expected each separate train. I waited for the fall of the signal as one expects a clap of thunder in the middle of a storm, and as there was no escape, either in the house or grounds, I felt that unless I got out of the place itself entirely, I should be found in my morning-room, seated on the floor, with straws in my hair, *à l'Ophelia*, a willing and ready candidate for a place in any lunatic asylum which was far enough away from the haunts of men to ensure a certain amount of peace, at least, from the raving, roaring, rattling rail. There are other suburban terrors which are to be dreaded, and which should certainly be looked out for before one settles down, if one is in the least susceptible to noise, as no one knows what torture can be given one by apparently innocent means. In delightful Shortlands, where I think the suburbs are as near perfection as a clay soil will allow, everyone in my day used to keep dogs as necessary protections from the ubiquitous tramp, and should one dog feel called upon to assert himself, all followed suit with the most exemplary precision. Then our next-door neighbour not only kept crowing and blatant cocks, but a flock of ever-increasing pigeons, and these dear creatures used to spend their happiest hours among my chimney-pots, moaning, cooing and groaning in the melancholy way they affect until they nearly drove me wild, and I had to appeal to the owner, who, with unprecedented goodness, got rid of them and so saved me from an untimely fate. But that was Shortlands. What shall I say for another suburb, where toy houses stand on quarter acres of ground, enclosed by breast-high fences, and where the fact of being a neighbour seems to ensure you as much annoyance as can be given in a short space of time? Where the ridiculous gates to the far more ridiculous 'carriage approaches' (see house agents' advertisements) are slammed one after another by the tradespeople, tramps, postmen and other fashionable folk who use these approaches. There, ensconced in a tub, close to each side of each fence, reposes an enormous dog, with a bark to match, who could protect all the silver and diamonds in the world—which are *not* to be found in what I call 'Pooter Parade' (for the origin of which name please read 'Nobody's Diary' in *Punch*)—where the servants hang out the clothes and themselves at the same time, if they can make investigations into their next-door neighbours' affairs; and which said suburb is finally and liberally furnished with children whose shrieks of pleasure or pain rend the air from dewy morn until late eve and sometimes later still. There when one tries to sleep it is between the barks of the vigilant hounds, the slamming of the gate by an irate tramp sent empty away, or else disappointed by a useless visit to the unprotected garden; for, raked fore and aft as it is by the populace, a lock seems a farce, especially when it would mean sending a maid down to the gates every time someone wanted to come in. Indeed the gates are so easily climbed, that any amount of locks would be no protection, and where one exists, protected yet unprotected in a childish degree which would be laughable were it not so disagreeable. For anyone could 'burgle' any of those villa residences had he an ounce of pluck, or did he not know quite well that the entire contents of the whole row would not pay him for his trouble, and would certainly not be worth the risk he ran from an irate householder and his dog roused from their uneasy slumbers to the protection of *Lares et Penates*.

I have tried life, more or less, for about twelve years in the suburbs of London, both north and south, and I have come to the conclusion that if we have a carriage and can therefore live a certain distance from the rail, and if we can put at least three acres of ground round our house, and pass moreover a series of regulations, *viâ* the new Parish Councils perhaps, for suburban etiquette, or better still, if rules for the behaviour of one neighbour towards another could be drawn up, the southern and south-western suburbs of London are the best places in the world to be in, for ordinary middle-class folk whose best days are over and who yet must be within touch of town for business purposes. These, therefore, should be ransacked by the house-hunter before he allows his eye to wander further afield. Though it must be remembered that the trains to such parts of the globe are maddening,—the only difference between an express and an ordinary train being that one waits outside a station and the other inside,— and the smallest amount of snow or fog will disorganise the traffic altogether, yet they do go to civilized parts of London, while those from the northern portions do not. The southern trains too, kindly drop one, say at Holborn, London Bridge, Charing Cross, or Victoria, and do not insist on one's returning by precisely the same station one arrived at: an immense advantage that one has only to be deprived of to comprehend instantly all it means.

If one goes to the northern suburbs of London, one is dropped at Euston, King's Cross, or, worse still, Liverpool Street, valuable stations for some men, but utterly useless for women; at least I never found them any good to me. True, one has the delightful trains and perfect manners of the Euston officials and I daresay the other northerners are as good, but I don't know much about them. Still, the punctuality and good service are all one has to set against the other drawbacks, which are, to my mind, more than a set off for the fact that the trains are good and punctual. These other drawbacks are that some of the northern suburbs are at least twenty years behind the south in conveniences and comforts; that the people who live there are not to be compared with the southrons, and that there is an almost unbroken surface of clay from London to beyond Harrow and Bushey; and that above all, unless one has a really large place, one must be so close to one's neighbours owing to the way the ground is arranged for building, that one nearly dies of them, and that it is almost, if not quite, impossible to keep out of the reach of the railway, which is far more ubiquitous there than it is in other parts of the regions round London. Then too there are no advantages in the way of amusement, while the distance of the stations available in London from the theatres makes the matinee question much more serious than it is from a more reachable spot.

If young married people think of settling in the suburbs, they should weigh the *pros* and *cons* thereof most seriously before determining their course. There is very little actual society in the suburbs, but what there is, is perhaps more real than the rush and hurry of London; and if a woman wants to do positive, helpful work, and to live a really healthy, morally and mentally healthy life, and a man cares for his home, his garden and his games, the couple will be much better off there than elsewhere. But if they love London, as Londoners do love their native city, if they are strong, 'in the swim,' 'smart,' or whatever is the proper designation for those who are really given over to society, let them stay where they are. For them a back attic in Belgravia is sweeter than a palace in the suburbs; for one never acclimatises, one only withers, and the husband, tired with that dreadful 'catching of trains,' has no mind for going out, while the wife may be done up by shopping in town, or be wearied out by mere dulness, and life will resolve itself into a procession of grey days and grimmer nights, and quickly, far too quickly, the *ménage* will become unbearable, and rupture, sooner or later, will ensue.

For, remember, if really intellectual or interesting people are found in the suburbs, they are, as I have just remarked, too tired from the day's work to be available for society purposes. But the majority of suburban residents is made up from young married folk, and dreary, common-place, middle-aged ones, made dreary by their surroundings, and by their enforced severance from their more fortunate fellow-creatures. For unless they have real fondness for literature, or for helping among the charities and churches, and have tastes of their own which render them superior to their actual surroundings, there is literally nothing to keep them alert and alive.

Whatever suburb is selected, it should include amongst its residents some family in a good position, to whom the new-comer is known or is known of. If the fresh resident has no introductions, his fate is sealed; the best people don't call, and should some years elapse before the acquaintance is made that might have been so pleasant if made at first, the relationship can never be a cordial one. Rightly or wrongly, the feeling exists that such an out-of-date visit is not worth thinking of, and it rarely becomes what it might have been, had not the untoward delay slipped in between.

The suburbs could be so different, nay, in isolated cases are so different, that I long for the residents to realise all they are throwing away, all one learns too late to really profit by the lessons. In Shortlands people used to be exceptionally fortunate, for there existed in our day an intellectual headquarter, where the 'hall-mark' was or was not affixed, as might be. Don't please think I mean myself; no one who knew Shortlands would think I could be such an idiot, and all will realise to whom I refer. Some years after we left, that pleasant house was broken up by the death of the founder; yet as long as it existed it was invaluable, because it acted like a fountain of living water and kept everything, as it were, fresh and young. In all suburbs there should be something of the same kind, someone of real and acknowledged tact and talent, who should know who is who and what is what, who could recognise pleasant, educated folk and give them a helping hand, and whose house should issue the 'hall-mark' which should make all these said pleasant, educated people able to feel they can be, an' they choose, members of the circle that ought to exist everywhere as a means of keeping souls alive and happy. A harder task, by the way, than the equally necessary one of keeping bodies in a similar state, and quite as important. Indeed, the one depends very much upon the other, as doctors are among the very first to recognise nowadays. In the olden times, and given a good man and a clever woman, the hall-mark used to be affixed by the rectory or vicarage, and whether the new-comers went to church or stayed away settled the question at once and for all time. But now matters are entirely changed, and the Church has little or nothing to do with the social standing of Brown and Jones and Smith. So if the suburb is to be successful, it must possess someone who, by right of brains and an assured position, can bring together the real folk and leave alone the dull, stupid ones who love gossip, and hate books and art and pictures, and so ensure an intellectual centre, which, once formed, would make any suburb as delightful as Shortlands was, in the days when I knew it well, and no doubt still is.

Given the suburbs then, the be-all and end-all of this little book is to teach the dwellers there, by choice or force, how best to avail themselves of the advantages which do exist, and which could be multiplied a thousandfold, did people know how to set to work. That I did not, makes me the best person in the world to teach others, because I have learned by experience and am therefore capable of imparting the knowledge I acquired too late to be able to use it myself. Therefore let me insist that the would-be suburban resident recognise first his duty to himself in the selection of his suburb, and then, secondly, his duty towards his neighbour. If he is close enough to him to be a nuisance he should consider him as much as he considers himself, while he bears in mind that there must be a social head to whom he will loyally give help, should he himself be anxious to wear the 'hall-mark' that will give all, rich and poor alike, the right to be a members of society, where pleasantness and culture suffice to ensure a hearty welcome.

The suburban's duty towards himself consists in selecting a suburb where the train shall land him nearest to his work in town; in selecting a good and reasonable house, and in finding out what amusements and occupations are available for his wife and daughters; and, if he has small children, what schools or teachers are likely to be useful in the matter of education. His duty to his neighbour may not be so briefly summed up, but consists in many little and worrying observances which are ridiculous indeed to the dwellers in London, and in more favoured and larger spots; but I, alas! can feelingly enumerate some of the items which go to make up a whole.

The first duty is undoubtedly to abstain from keeping a dog which must be tied up either day or night. The second is to bar crowing cocks and crooning pigeons; one can be quite happy without pigeons, and cocks can't crow if they can't get their heads up high enough to do so, neither are they necessary inhabitants of a small back-garden. Hanging out the clothes should be a penal offence, as should be the slamming of gates, an offensive dust-bin, ill-bred servants, and screaming children, while the utterer of long unchecked yells should be at once fined or punished as an offender against the community; for children can't too soon be taught to know their duties towards their neighbours, the while they learn self-control and the undoubted fact that screams and cries are not necessary items in anyone's bringing up. Then carpets and rugs should not be shaken and dusted after ten o'clock, and without some idea of the way of the wind. The letters sent to 'Ivy Dene,' and delivered at 'Deneside,' should be at once given up at their real destination, and should not be detained until the postman is caught by chance on one of his hurried plunges down the 'carriage approach,' which, by the way, won't exist in our model suburb. Moreover, when Jones gives a party and doesn't ask Smith and Brown, it should be a matter of honour to both neighbours that they don't disport themselves unduly, in their gardens at the same time making pointed remarks about Jones's guests and entertainment which cannot fail to be heard all over the somewhat limited space at Jones's disposal. Indeed the whole duty of a suburban resident is to treat his neighbour as himself in the matter of conduct, but not to know him personally if he can in any way and decently avoid doing so, for 'beware to whom you give the key of your back door,' says a wise old proverb, and one gives it away very freely when one is on the intimate terms one must be if one knows one's real neighbour in the suburbs in the very smallest degree. Endless friction can be caused by the mere *va et vient* of tennis balls; or by ignoring the fact that no one wants the same people at all the small parties given in a locality, the size of which must govern in a measure at all times the amount of folks bidden to them. Servants who can chatter over the fences are also a fertile source of misunderstanding. So unless specially clever and sensible folks dwell beside one, it is best to know nothing of them in any shape or form if one wants the peace, without which Paradise itself would fail to charm, and deprived of which, the suburban resident realises all too quickly what being in the antipodes of Paradise might very probably mean.

Then when these duties are fulfilled the next one is to discover of what manner of men is composed, and what is the record of, the new parish council or local board which may govern the special district; and another is to find if the 'Infectious Diseases Notification Act' has been adopted or not. These two things are most important, for given a good local authority one knows that while the rates don't rise unduly, yet proper care is taken that all matters are up to date, which they can never be in a place where the 'Infectious Diseases Act' is not enforced; neither can health be found where jerry building reigns unchecked, bad meat is passed over casually as not too bad to eat (just as if all edibles should not resemble Caesar's wife and be above the smallest suspicion), where the water is bitterly hard, and not either soft or softened, and where, in fact, everything is what ought not to be, and nothing is that should be to ensure a maximum of health with a careful regard to the spending of the ratepayers' money. Then one very necessary hint to suburban residents is to see that in taking a new house the road by which it may stand, or by which it is reached, is properly 'made up,' and duly taken over by the authorities. Especially should this be the case if the house stands at a corner, albeit, for many reasons, a corner house should not be selected. Some feeble folk imagine such a situation means bad luck. Well! so it does in a measure; for being at a corner, one gets all the winds that blow on all sides, one's front garden is filled with paper, straw and debris of all kinds, brought into it by these said eddying winds; the dust fills our rooms and makes our curtains black before their time, and one gets a double assortment of noises both of vehicles and people; while, if we all too late discover the road has not been 'made up,' and 'taken over,' we have not only the front but a side piece to pay for, and in consequence have three times the money to disburse that is expected of our neighbours. Besides which, should snow fall there are the side walks to clear as well as the front one; we have more wall or fence to keep in order, and, being less protected from the weather are less warm than we should have been had we had houses on both sides of us instead of only one house and a wide expanse of road, where often enough, school children play in a maddening manner, and where we get all the side noises as well as those which are to be found along the front. The soil of the suburb is again a thing to be thoroughly acquainted with before the tent is pitched finally and for all time thereon. I do not believe clay is or ever can be fit for anyone to reside upon, and nothing anyone can say will cause me to alter my opinion. True I know that London, the healthiest city in the world, is nearly all on clay, but then it has the advantage not only of perfect drainage, but of every other thing which can mitigate this fundamental drawback to perfect health; yet the fogs and the chill and the gloom which distinguish it might all be different, or, indeed, non-existent, were the soil of another character. Dearly as I loved Shortlands the clay there was always to be reckoned with, and made a long reckoning too, when all was told, for though roses flourished magnificently, children didn't, and coughs and colds were 'the only wear' once autumn began to spread the leaves and winter came up to finish the little business, clad in the usual garments of fog and mist, changed at times to other more 'seasonable' ones of frost and snow. Chalk is to be avoided by all rheumatic souls, or by those to whom rheumatism may arrive by right of inheritance, water in which chalk exists largely being a great help to bringing such an inheritance within easy grasp of the heir; but gravel and, I think, a certain measure of sand, are all right, while many trees should be fled from. Trees bring rain and insects, and mean damp; albeit, if we can only find a suburb where the gracious pine tree flourishes, we can dwell there without alarm. The pine-tree spells health always, and should be sought for as carefully as a family of *nouveaux riches* searches for its coat of arms, or some one thing that will link it on to someone else's noble ancestors in some way or another. Therefore should the seeker after a suburban residence arm himself with a geological map of the regions round London, and make many pilgrimages and inquiries before he finally chooses. He would be wise too if he could afford the time and money, to take rooms or a furnished house first in the locality which appeals to him most; but, if he can't do that, he should take in the local newspaper, for at least a month, and see what manner of conduct is reported there; what are the doings of the local authorities, the species of 'happenings' in the way of amusements and entertainments, and if he is bent on church, he should attend one or two services; while, if golf attracts him, and tennis is his only joy, he should see that both are attainable, and that the clubs are get-into-able and are not either beyond his pocket or whatever may be his special social status.

Once these items are all satisfactorily settled, and the suburb really selected, the tug of war may be fairly considered to have begun. The suburb is found, but how about the special house? Of course 'eligible residences' will abound, albeit in any good and favoured places they are not as plentiful by half as one could wish, so that nothing should be done in a hurry.

The local tradespeople, as well as the house-agents (generally very broken reeds these last too) should be taken into one's confidence, and if a specially good house is to be let in a month or two it should be stalked as carefully as one stalks a stag of price, and with as much cunning. Too great eagerness means a large premium, and all the last tenant's awful fixtures; too little means someone else slipping in before one, and bearing off the coveted prize under one's very eyes.

Much as one likes the idea of a real new, clean house, where no one has ever died, or had scarlet fever, small-pox, or diphtheria, and where virgin walls and untouched rooms leave one a free hand as regards decoration and furniture, it is better, if possible, to take some place out of which a 'good family' has been obliged to move for some true and reasonable cause, such as a loss or increase of income, or an increase in the requirements of the family. If a new house is chosen, it is absolutely necessary that some honest and tried sanitary authority should be called in from a distance: a local man cannot possibly give an unbiassed opinion; and he should thoroughly examine the system of drains; all pipes should be disconnected from the soil-pipes, and all sanitary arrangements should be placed on the outside of the house. I do not mean apart from the house itself, but built on at one side, so that drainage is simplified immensely and reduced to one area. One where the soil-pipe can be thoroughly ventilated and easily got at should it be necessary to examine the drains, to repair them, or to discover that they are all in good and working order. They should also be capable of being constantly and copiously flushed with a good stream of water, while all pipes connected with the water supply should be protected from the weather, and also easily reached, else will they burst at the least provocation, and cause frost and cold to be doubly cursed, because of their untoward action upon one's domestic arrangements. If the house has been lived in, confidential relations should be established with the outgoing tenant unless he has any interest in getting the house off his hands; in that case human nature being weak, one can but recollect he wants to part with it. But if he have ended his lease and be genuinely anxious to remain yet cannot for a reasonable cause, it were well to ask him frankly about the wants, requirements, and moods of the special abode, for houses want humouring just as do human beings, and very often one only finds out the virtues when the vices have caused one to throw up the sponge, and once more set out on our nomadic passing through this life.

If we select and take a new house before we attempt our decorations let us instal a caretaker. Ay! even with her grimy self and her still more grimy goods and bronchial family, heavy with the continual colds inseparable from living in empty houses and never anywhere else; and let us see by ocular demonstration that she keeps going the large and splendid fires which should be in all the rooms even before we contemplate how we are going to treat them. For until the house has been exposed to the ordeal by warmth we cannot possibly tell whether we shall have to begin by relaying shrunken floors; putting the ever useful 'Slater's Patent' round every door and window, and whether it were not well to transfer certain doors from left to right or *vice versa*, because of the position of fire and window, which can only be really determined when we see how the fire burns, and from which side comes most of the almost certain draught. Thus too are tested the young and untried chimneys, which, should they smoke, are to be examined by a practical man before anything else can be done. They may smoke through faulty construction. In this case new grates must be had from Haines & Co., 83 Queen Victoria Street, who have a grate that can easily deal with this desperate strait. Or they may require tall chimney-pots, or a mere 'blower,' which is best when made of a clear thick sheet of glass. In any case, they must be treated at once. A smoky chimney is death to one's decorations, spoils one's temper, and one's white curtains and new cretonnes, and gives the maids cause for dissatisfaction, the while we take a hatred at once to the house and always remember its unkind reception of us, however well it may behave to us when we find ourselves better acquainted with its little ways. It would not be an auspicious manner of beginning an acquaintance should some would-be friend receive us with sulks and a turned-away countenance, which might be shyness, and is certainly bad mannered: I question much if we should ever reach friendship should our advances be met in a similar way! In such a manner does a smoky chimney make one feel towards the house it is a part of, and once we are received with smoke in our own domain, we can never really forget or forgive a reception we should not have had, had we kept up good fires before we entered into possession thereof. When the house is warmed, we can proceed to deal with each portion thereof as our tastes and our purses permit; but we must never allow anything which really offends our own special taste to remain; neither must we be talked into taking anything we don't like. If we don't know our own minds in these days, there are advisers to be had on whom reliance can be placed. But if we have the least idea of what we want, let us get it. It is our own house after all, and it is right it should represent us, and not other folk. At the same time many people who can recognise beauty and comfort when they see it, get bewildered by quantities; and unable to select between them cannot secure loveliness, and are equally unable somehow to recognise how comfort can be obtained.

'How do you keep this room up to 60 degrees?' once said a doctor to me, when I was inhabiting, *pro tem.*, a so-called furnished house in the depth of the winter. 'I had a child dying here of bronchitis last winter, and, try how they would, his people couldn't raise the temperature to above 50 degrees, although his life depended on it.'

'Ah,' said I, 'they doubtless left it as they found it. I didn't. I have covered the gaping stained "surround" with felt. I have hung curtains inside and outside the rickety door and instead of feeble wisps of muslin to the windows I have four good thick curtains besides long thin ones. That's all the secret; and I never burn gas as you see, while my fires last twice as long as they did before the alterations.'

'Oh, I wish I had known all that before,' said the doctor, 'for neither I nor the parents could find out the cause of the cold.'

A little thing which will illustrate better than any amount of further description what I mean by saying that people don't always know how to obtain comfort though they can appreciate it when found.

CHAPTER II

HALLS AND PASSAGES

IF we wish to make a complete conquest of the special suburban residence we are about to circumvent, there is no doubt whatever that the first battle of all has to be fought and won on the very doorstep. Nay sometimes one has to commence the conflict before we reach as far as that, for have we not the 'carriage sweep' to tackle and the slamming gate to minister to before reaching the front door? If we are cursed with the 'approach,' all we can do is to make the gate as inoffensive as we can, for alas! we must keep it or we shall have our front garden a gathering ground for all the curs in the neighbourhood. But we must e'en remove the latch altogether, and line the place where it was with indiarubber, and put a couple of stout indiarubber springs on the house side of the gate, which should have an inner lining of wire-netting, and a head-trimming of barbed wire, or else of rough nails, to prevent the demon boy seating himself thereon. Then, if by firm refusals to allow tramps to come up, and by never giving them one farthing—or indeed anything save a bread ticket redeemable at the nearest baker's shop, and which, ten to one, we shall find torn up in our 'avenue,'—we can induce them to mark our gate with some secret sign, which means we are unspeakable brutes and not good even for a 'little hot water,' we shall have ensured ourselves a certain amount of quiet, and shall, at all events, have begun our campaign in the right way. Our gate we should paint some good solid colour, and Indian red is a good shade with green hedges and trees about us, as is also a special shade of dark olive green. Then the name of the house should be painted on in white, *not* gilded letters, and if we put as well 'Please shut this gate quietly' on both sides of the top bar, we shall find that we at least are no longer noise-makers in general, and, as far as our special gate is concerned, the great slamming question is replied to satisfactorily.

I may seem to dwell unduly on the matter of noise, but I can assure my readers that every preventable noise is both a sin against themselves and also against their neighbours. They may be in rude health and inclined to jeer at all I say, but the day will come when their heads will ache and their nerves bother them and when noise will torture them, and then they will wish devoutly that they had legislated at first for peace, for they certainly won't get it when they have not the strength to insist on it. I say preventable noise, and most noises are that, for even the wretched piano in the schoolroom can be placed in such a position that it only worries those to whom it belongs; while the person who encourages barrel-organs or screaming children, should be at once sent to the wilds of America, no other place being large enough to hold such a barbarian.

We know, of course, all English folk think their homes are their castles; well, if so, the castle should have appropriate surroundings. There is nothing much of the castle about a suburban residence, and the sooner this fact is realised the better for those who dwell therein and on both sides. Now, the carriage gate being painted and settled with, and arranged to be fastened back should we have many callers from three to six in summer, from three to five in winter, we can turn our attention to the front door. I have had to circumvent for myself and for many many other folk the ordinary suburban residence, and I have only in one case found the front door treated in a manner that showed me that the man who planned the house had the very smallest idea of what he was about. As a rule, the front door opens straight on the narrow passage called hall by courtesy, with the ladder-like flight of stairs going straight up at one side. Then just opposite the front door, and about eighteen or twenty feet from it, is the door of the third room, which becomes library, smoking-room, or even day-nursery or schoolroom, according to the tastes and the age and number of the owner's family, and nothing can be worse than this arrangement. But in the exception of which I speak, the hall ends at the front door portion in a wall, and the front door is placed opposite, as in the diagram on the next page, and thus the wind which enters when the front

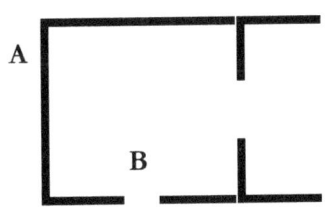

door is opened only circulates in the tiny vestibule, and is shut off from the hall and house by the inner door, beyond which is a small fireplace, so small as to be scarcely visible at all, yet large enough to ensure the equal temperature which means so much in this very evil-minded climate of ours. Now, it would not be an enormous expense, either to add the vestibule, or to make it by closing the ordinary entrance at A and opening one at B, while the vestibule could be shut off from the hall by curtains, should there be light enough to do without the extra window, or by a glazed screen, should light be otherwise an impossibility. In any case the gain to health would be enormous, while the comfort is of course at once ensured which is so absolutely necessary, and yet as a rule is so little understood. If one can have curtains, and expense is a great object, it is well to obtain from

Oetzmann a fretwork arch, which is made for this purpose, and which is nailed on the wall and to the ceiling, and is at once simple and effective. The rod the simplest brass one which can be procured, should go behind the arch, which should face towards the end wall, and curtains of Wallace's diamond serge should fall from the rod; there should be two full curtains, double, if possible, and edged with 'grip cord,' not ball-fringe. They will be constantly moved, and ball-fringe would soon spoil, while the cord is a hardy thing and capable of standing a certain amount of pulling about. As a rule the floor of the ordinary suburban hall is made from the roughest of boards which shrink apart coyly from each other as if they were youthful maidens at their first ball, but sometimes we are fortunate enough to come across tiles. And yet I don't know whether I should quite say fortunate! For sometimes the tiles are more frightful than I can describe, and are often cracked and irregular, while one can manage the boarded floor if one resolutely tackles it and determines that it shall not conquer one instead of being conquered itself. If one has tiles one should place two or three rugs over them, the Abingdon Carpet Company's charming 'Arts and Crafts' rugs for choice, made in the proper length and width for these places; but if one has not, the boards must first be stopped, planed and smoothed and ventilated, and then a plain cork carpet from Wallace, of Curtain Road, E.C. should be put down. This should be ventilated too, by piercing holes here and there with a gimlet, else dry-rot will ensue, a thing which once in possession is very difficult to get rid of, I can assure my readers. The cork carpet must be supplemented by rugs, and in any case the vestibule should be tiled with plain self-coloured tiles to harmonise with the decorations, for here would be shed the wet waterproofs and umbrellas of the way-worn traveller, who could then proceed towards the drawing-room undeterred by the despair that seizes one when one feels at a disadvantage owing to one's raiment. This feeling often prevents people paying that kindest call of all, the call on a wet, dreary day, when we are dying with loneliness and boredom, and would give anything to see the friend who will not come because she would be 'too wet for the pretty room,' and 'so dirty, she would really be ashamed to enter anyone's house.'

Now, with the sensible short tweed skirt and tweed undergarments, which fortunate present-day damsels don unknown and unchecked, and a good plain, yet pretty waterproof, anyone is weather-tight; and if the parlour-maid pops the umbrella into the beaten iron ring for that purpose placed behind the front door, and hangs the waterproof up in Wallace's handy P. T. C. wardrobe in another corner; and if the boots are carefully wiped on the mat placed in the sunken place in front of the door, the visitor enters the room spotless and as dry as if she had just emerged from her own house or from Lady Gorgeous Midas's brand new brougham. The tiled floor should have upon it a pretty thick rug lined with American leather: one can be bought for about 8s. 9d. at Treloar's: an outlay that no one need mind, but that ensures once more a certain amount of comfort.

The front door should, of course, never be grained, and it ought in these days to be quite unnecessary for me even to hint at such a thing. But mighty is the 'local decorator,' beloved of the suburbs, and his counsels will undoubtedly prevail, unless we put down our foot very firmly indeed, and keep it resolutely in that special attitude. He will 'grain' the door if he can until doomsday, I am convinced, but my readers must be firm and dignified, and above all must they give their instructions in writing, and keep a duplicate signed by the 'decorator' (save the mark!), else will they find he has gone his own sweet way after all, and they have no redress whatever. It is an axiom that whatever colour is chosen for the hall that colour alone shall be on the front door, but it may be in a darker shade, while the vestibule can often be treated differently to the hall itself, though of course it should lead up to and harmonise with it. Let me describe what I mean. The special vestibule I am thinking of has a couple of small, diamond-paned windows, one at the end, one opposite the front door, and below this latter is a wide panel painted with a tiger-lily, and then a wide wooden seat which lifts up and holds carriage rugs, and on which anyone could sit did he or she come with a message or a note and require to wait an answer. Both windows have wide ledges on which stand pots holding palms or aspidistras, and all the paint on the inside of the front door and on the vestibule side of the glass screen-doors included, is a special, beautiful soft grey-blue shade. The panelled walls are the same colour; the curtains are soft yellow silk, and the ceiling proper is yellow and cream. On the floor are dull blue tiles and a Scinde rug, and in one corner is the umbrella-ring, which one can get at Shoolbred's for about 18s. 9d., and that is all. There is no room for the P. T. C. here, and the waterproofs are taken at once into the servants' room to be hung up and dried, but it would be much better were there a corner wardrobe, only, alas! one can't make space where one doesn't possess it.

The screen is made somewhat like this. The top and side panels are all of leaded glass, as far as the brackets which hold pots for palms. The tops of the doors are more leaded glass, and all the base is wood painted on the vestibule side, the soft grey-blue spoken of before, and on the other a specially soft and deep 'real ivory.' The dado is of ivory, gold, and black Japanese leather paper, and the paper above is one of Smee & Cobay's, and is a cunning blend of green and red, managed in such a way that the whole effect is a pinky red, which harmonises with the grey-blue, and is as original as it is undoubtedly most pleasant to contemplate. The stairs and all doors are curtained off with yellow diamond serge, and the passage—*i.e.* hall—is covered with plain green cork carpet, on which are laid rugs in which the grey-blue colour aforesaid predominates. Of course the ceiling is papered in yellow and white, and equally, of course, all the paint is one even surface of colour. Nothing can excuse picked out or striped and embellished paint: nothing! Genius is better employed on better work, and even genius is out of place in making ornamental that which after all is only going to be part of a harmonious whole, and merely a background to ourselves and our possessions. Therefore must there be plain paint everywhere, and no cornice should be more than a moulded band, merely coloured a plain cream or ivory colour. If the front door and the doors in the vestibule screen are not above suspicion of draughts, they should be at once surrounded with Slater's patent draught-excluders, which can be procured anywhere almost, but surely at Shoolbred's or Whiteley's; for nothing is more trying than a draught. Have as much air and proper ventilation as possible. Have a vestibule window open for some time of the day in winter and all day long in summer, and have the staircase window open as well: a house that can't have a thorough current of air cannot be a healthy one. But do not allow the insidious draught, and the cold and unwarmed halls and passages, which are ubiquitous save in a large house possessing a big, square hall, where one usually finds a good fireplace. However, one should manage somehow to make a fireplace there, ay, even if one can have nothing better than the small, round, moveable stove called the 'Ideal,' which burns patent fuel, and can be taken away at any moment. It should be placed on an iron corner bracket rather raised above the floor, and a guard should be round it, so that dresses could not come in contact with it. But one should never be tempted from the paths of virtue by the charms of oil stoves, for they always smell and are detestable, no matter what anyone says; for though they should not, of course, if properly cleaned and attended to, proper cleanliness and care mean personal attention in a small household, and I cannot think how anyone can touch oil, or whatever has held it without a shudder. There is a smell about paraffin that, let us 'shatter the stove as we will,' continues to cling about it and us in a way that is enough to make us and our friends very ill indeed. It's an unnecessary smell, too. If we can't depend on the maids, we must see to our own lamps, but we need not have stoves. They give a poor heat at best, and at worst—but there is no need to harrow our feelings by dwelling on that side of the picture. Be sure that whenever we can have real fires, we should have them, and that no house can be warm, and therefore healthy, if we have no fire in the passage. It need be only a wee one. It can be kept in for hours by using briquettes and small coal judiciously, and as it prevents colds and consequent suffering, and very probably doctors' bills, it need not be omitted on the score of expense. Once see to the draught-excluder and the hall fire, we shall save in the sitting-room fires too, which are often twice as wasteful as they need be, because we pile them up to warm the bitter air that rushes in when the door is opened, and because the ceaseless draughts from doors and windows drive the rushing heat up the chimney and make the coal burn out doubly as fast as it otherwise would. Then too there is no labour about the modern small tiled fireplace. It is cleaned and laid in less than five moments, and indeed were we sensible about our houses, we should not have half the bother with our maids that some of us have, because we would minimise the amount of work by labour-saving appliances, instead of making it double what it need be, as we all of us do, more especially in those suburban houses, where, after all, the labour question is one of the most burning problems that the female part of the population has to discuss at its weekly gatherings on its special afternoons at home.

    The hall grate should be on the smallest scale possible, should have a plain wooden mantel and small over-mantel consisting of a wooden frame and a slip of bevelled looking-glass, and should have tiles for a hearth and a surround, and should be provided with a high guard similar to those found in all nurseries, but in brass, not in common painted wire. On the mantel we could put one or two framed photographs and about four glasses for flowers, and also a small clock, should the hall not be sufficiently large to allow us to have the proper tall one there; but great care should be taken not to overdo the ornaments here especially, for a hall gathers dust in a dreadful manner, and too many ornaments mean dirt, and therefore should in no way be encouraged. The walls of the hall should have pictures on them; there is no doubt about that, and good autotypes and Burne-Jones's photographs from Mr Hollyer of 9 Pembroke Square, W., are the best to have. They should be framed in the simple reeded frames sold by the Autotype Company, New Oxford Street, and should be hung judiciously. The lowest should just, and only just, escape the dado-rail, the highest should be only a couple of inches above it at the outside. There should, of course, be no pictures whatever in the vestibule portion of the hall, neither in the hall itself should there be any brackets for china, nor over-doors on which pots and vases can be placed, for the maid must always get the steps to dust these places and, in consequence, dusting, is, at the best very seldom, at the worst never done. But over every door in the halls and passages must be placed *portières* of some kind or other. I have come to the conclusion that a couple of curtains is the best arrangement for this, if the doors open into the rooms, as they generally do in a small hall; if not, of course the rod, which opens and shuts with the door, and which Burnett sells for 4s. 6d. complete, must be used. The pair of curtains allows the servant to hold one back for the visitor's entrance as she opens the door, but they must be crossed at the top by putting the last hook on each curtain in the ring that comes last on the one belonging to its fellow; this prevents them from gaping open, and always keeps them in place. Suppose each curtain has six hooks, one puts five belonging to the left-hand curtain on the left-hand set of rings; in the sixth, one puts hook No. 1 of the right-hand curtain; hook No. 6 of the left-hand curtain goes into hook No. 1 of the right-hand one; the other five rings are filled by the remaining five hooks then on the right-hand curtain, and this ensures the curtains remaining always in their place in the most satisfactory way possible. The best material for hall curtains is undoubtedly Wallace's diamond serge, and it should be lined with sateen the same colour as that chosen for the curtains, and should be edged with grip-cord. The glazed surface of the sateen resists the dust, and the curtains should always be unhooked once a week and shaken out of doors, and the poles and rings rubbed over with the new Selvyt cloths, which are admirable, and far surpass the ordinary duster, as they polish as well as remove extraneous matter and dirt. This is the work of the housemaid, who is responsible for all dusting in the hall, and also for all brushing and shaking; the washing of the steps, cork carpet, etc., being the duty of the kitchen-maid, should one be kept; or else of the 'tweeny-maid,' who takes, in a measure, the kitchen-maid's place in the ordinary small-sized establishment. One word now about this said cork carpet, and the best way to treat it, for it really is a very important matter indeed. People should never allow themselves to be talked into buying the orthodox and hideous-patterned linoleum, which gives a hopelessly '*bourgeois*' appearance to any house, and at once puts a stop to anything like artistic decoration. 'The pattern going through to the back, as it does, ensures that it can never wear off,' says one person; 'have the beautiful linoleum which imitates parqueterie,' remarks another, regardless of the fact that such imitation is as vulgar as it is ugly. Why! it would be an advantage to me that the pattern should wear off, a pattern being generally a mistake on any hall floor; and, therefore, should the hall be untiled, or not made of the silent wood blocks which are the ideal component parts of any floor, and which are not likely therefore to be found in any suburban residence, one should be resolute, and refuse flatly to have anything at all but the soft-coloured cork carpet, which we can supplement with rugs. I am aware that at first one feels as if one were going mad over my pet material, for then every footmark shows, and every atom of dirt is visible, but I prefer to be able to see dirt, in order to ensure its speedy removal. Still if at first we give the cork carpet one thorough good rub with linseed oil and turpentine, and one only, all we need to do afterwards is to have it washed over with warm water, or milk and water. Soap should never be used on any account whatever, and then if once a week it has a real polish with beeswax and turpentine, it will wear for ever, and, after the first, will not unduly agitate us by bringing into prominence the erring footmarks of ourselves and our friends. But, of course, it must always be supplemented by rugs. Then we have an ideal hall covering, for the rugs can be taken up and shaken daily, and so is cleanliness ensured, and without that the house cannot possibly be habitable at all. On no account, not even in houses where 'expense is no object,' should a fitted carpet be allowed in the halls and passages, for it is utterly impossible to keep such an arrangement even decently clean. Think of the traffic in a hall! the muddy boots, the paws of the dear dogs (and everyone should have an *un*chained dog, it's the chained-up victims that are the terrors of the suburbs), and the drippings from wet umbrellas and garments, and renounce carpets there for evermore. Besides which, we have to remember the fact that it is almost impossible to sweep out any corners in rooms or halls, and that should the housemaid attempt to do so, she only knocks great pieces off the paint in her endeavours, and finally has to resort to a damp duster to pick up the 'fluff' which congregates there. Damping woollen carpets is one of the easiest methods of procuring a visit from the fatal moth, so should not be resorted to unless we are quite at our wits' end.

The ordinary suburban staircase is another of the things we have to approach with fear and trembling. As a rule, Jacob's ladder has suggested its design, and it is so proud of its appearance that it thrusts itself on our notice the instant we enter the house. In this case we can only grin and bear it, the while we make its long expanse of open balustrade and wooden understructure as bearable as we can by covering in the first with Eastern dhurries or Khelim curtains, and filling in any panels in the latter with Japanese leather paper, which is invaluable for this purpose. But should it be modestly stationed at one side, as has been the position of the three staircases which have been my portion in the suburban residences I have dwelt in most complainingly; then one can curtain them off better with the same arrangement of a fretwork arch I described when writing about the vestibule; or by a couple of stronger arches which one can get at Wallace's, one of which encloses the stair, and the other leads to the back premises and lavatories and cloak places. These arches are of course, curtained, and so the ordinary visitor sees nothing save the sitting-room doors or door and the hall itself, and is spared those awe-striking glimpses into unsuitable spots, which are all too often exposed guilelessly to the unhappy and much-embarrassed guest, who neither wishes to see into the parlour-maid's pantry, nor to view a vast line of old hats, waterproofs and tennis rackets, and who much prefers to remain ignorant of these and many other secret arrangements of the innermost recesses of our home.

Now not only are the position and design of the staircase more annoying than I can say, but the stairs themselves are, as a rule, simply too painful for words. They generally consist of a series of short, sharp ascents, and are never by any chance low and broad, as a self-respecting stair should most undoubtedly be, and are moreover so extremely narrow and sharp at the edges that they are warranted to wear through any stair carpet in less than a twelvemonth, save perhaps a pile carpet, and that they will ruin in a couple of years at the outside. No one can alter either the steepness or narrowness of the stairway. Alas! they are both past praying for, but if the sharp edges are circumvented by carpet pads sold by any good upholsterer for a few pence or manufactured at home out of curled paper enclosed in linen covers, and made to resemble a very small, thick cushion, and if we put carpet felt under the carpet we shall find the carpet itself wear decently at anyrate, especially if we see it is carefully moved once a month in such a way that the portion that was at the top one month lives at the bottom the next, reversing this same position once more when the time comes to move it again. I have often remarked that there is no such thing as a cheap stair carpet, and that the cheapest article at first is the dearest in the end, and I have seen no reason to alter my opinion. Pile with only a small design as pattern and no fidgety border, is the best thing in the world, and can be bought at from 4s. 11d. to 7s. 9d. a yard. Next to pile comes Brussels at about 4s. 6d. Then comes Wallace's 'Dunelm' at about 4s., and, finally, a new, self-coloured, all-wool material called 'Roysse,' sold by the Abingdon Carpet Company at 2s. 3d. three-quarter width—the ordinary stair width— and at 2s. 11d. a yard wide. Lower than this I cannot for one moment advise even the most impecunious among us to go; neither can I advise the 'bargains' and 'odd lengths' of pile and Brussels that are often obtainable at really good shops. If they are bargains as far as material and make are concerned, they are absolutely hideous, and are only got rid of because even the British taste has refused them; and if they are odd lengths we cannot ever match them, and that means replacing the whole carpet should an accident happen to one small part of it, which we could have replaced in one moment had we bought a proper carpet. Such an one as is always kept in stock by most of the best shops in London, the owners of which have learned that a good and pretty thing is a joy for ever, and that once it is pronounced such it can be always recommended and brought forward, not because it is the 'last new thing,' but because it is old, and has been well and truly tried and not found wanting.

The upstairs passages should be treated to more cork carpet and rugs, and under no circumstances must a 'walk' of carpet be allowed, neither may the rugs be put down in a wearisome, unbroken line unless the passage is very narrow and allows of no deviating from the straight path. If there be a landing, as a rule two rugs are required, and in the passage the rugs can be put one after the other in a somewhat similar way, less, as I remarked before, the passage is very narrow. In that case a 'vestibule rug' must be procured either from Shoolbred, Hewetson or the Abingdon Carpet Company. These can be had in lengths of about 6 feet by 4 wide, and 9 feet by the same width, while there are both longer and wider rugs to be procured, but then the passage should be long enough to allow of there being two in use, if not more, when they can be placed in any position save in a long, straight line.

The doors of the upstairs rooms must always be securely curtained, and here one wide, full curtain should suffice. There is not the continual exit and entrance to these chambers there is to the downstairs rooms, so then one curtain upstairs will be enough. These should be kept in place by putting the end rings past the bracket on which the brass rod rests, then the last hooks on the curtain are put into them, thus ensuring that the curtains are always kept drawn. Anyone who has passed by a vista of open bedroom doors, left open when the owners have, at the sound of the gong, rushed downstairs to meals in too great a hurry to put their rooms tidy, will not need to have impressed upon them the fact that it is absolutely necessary to decency to have *portières* which fall into place behind the person who leaves his or her bedroom door open, and so discloses to all comers the ravages which getting up too often leaves in view. It is a good thing also to conceal the entrance to the bathroom and lavatories by a curtain, which should depend from a beaten iron arm which stretches straight out into the passage. This arm can be procured from Bartholomew & Fletcher for about 18s. 6d., while the curtain should be heavy; printed velveteen made double and fan-edged making an absolutely perfect if somewhat expensive curtain. Godfrey Giles has a charming velveteen, which is a mixture of blue and green. Wallace has a beautiful yellow and cream one, and Smee & Cobay have these velveteens in most colours, notably in a rich and exquisite red, which it is a pleasure to look at, and which also wears extremely well, even in windows where the sun has a certain amount of actual power, and is never really kept out at all.

Any cornice upstairs as well as down must be coloured 'cream' or 'real ivory,' and the ceilings here as elsewhere must be papered with some simple, inexpensive paper, in a colour which harmonises with the decorations. And now let me impress upon my readers that even if they have only taken their suburban villa on the usual tentative three years' lease: which is so rarely renewed: it is always worth while to make their surroundings charming, even should they not remain in the house after the first term of the three, seven or twenty-one years' lease is over. First because if the lessee and the owner combined would take trouble to ensure beauty and comfort, I am quite certain that moving would not be as continual as it is at present. The trouble taken over the house would endear it to the dwellers therein, while the comfort would cause them to think twice before they deprived themselves of it; for once let one's roots really strike home, and no one who has not tried it can tell how difficult it is to drag them out of even an uncongenial soil. While from a congenial one! well, there is nothing on earth so hard to do and so fearfully difficult to bear, and no after-delights can cause these wounds really and truly to heal! Secondly, dear readers, it is always worth while to have beautiful and harmonious surroundings, ay, even for a few months and even if we have to leave them. For in this latter case, we shall have left them as an art legacy to our successor, who will not be very difficult to find if we leave behind us charming papers and appropriate decorations to mark where we have once made our home!

Of course each individual hall requires individual treatment, and it would be well-nigh impossible to lay down any hard and fast rules to be followed implicitly; but a dado, a real not a sham one, is an absolute necessity in any narrow hall, and no one should be afraid of one of coloured paper, bold in hue as in design, for a large, bold pattern makes a small place appear larger, and real colour must always be a pleasure, which a muddled, pale and timid tint can never be. A dado could be of wood, if the lease is long enough, and the purse too, to allow of it. In this case Godfrey Giles's 'gœhring' material and 'Glastonbury' panelling will suit those who cannot afford oak. Arras cloth, with a pattern printed on it is beautiful, especially if hung like the old-fashioned arras used to be, to resemble a gathered curtain. Then I am devoted to the plain, string-coloured matting, sold on purpose for dados at 10½d. a yard; and there are of course, anaglypta and Japanese leather paper always with us, while the printed arras cloth paper is a strong and good material which is not to be despised by any manner of means at all. In all cases there must be a real dado-rail, and the paper above, as indeed every single thing in the hall, should harmonise. I am devoted to a blue hall myself: the one described in the first part of the chapter can well be absolutely copied, while it should be remembered that a dark hall calls for yellow and cream, or red and cream a real, bold, sealing-wax red: let there be no mistake about the colour: and nothing should authorise the employment of either a green or a terra-cotta hall. Green can never be a success there, while terra-cotta spells fear and shows artistic hankerings which the owner is unable, or not bold enough to carry out. I am not devoted to any terra-cotta save some shades sold only by Liberty. I would never have even these, save in some bedrooms and an occasional, a very occasional, dining-room or library.

As a rule the lighting of the hall should be managed by placing first, in the vestibule, a gasalier in the very centre of the ceiling, where the gas should be enclosed in a bucket-shaped glass in a beaten-iron lantern frame; secondly, in the hall itself a similar treatment should be followed out, if the ceilings be high enough to allow of it: if not, side-brackets near the dining and drawing-room doors should be used. And finally more side-brackets should be upstairs, these again of beaten-iron, and with the same shaped glass. These can be bought very inexpensively of Shoolbred, while Messrs Strode & Company, of 48 Osnaburgh Street, Regent's Park, make beautiful and more expensive brackets and lanterns and lamps on the same lines.

There should be as little furniture as possible in the ordinary suburban hall or passage. The really necessary furniture has been described as placed in the vestibule; but, if we have room we should undoubtedly have a tall palm on a stand, a grandfather clock in one corner, a couple of chairs: tall, high-backed ones for choice: and, if possible, between the dining and drawing-room doors, which are often close together, or at anyrate close to the latter door, have a nice plain walnut table. This would hold the necessary bowl for cards left during the afternoon, and taken away every day, because keeping them seems like parading the amount and quality of one's friends; and, if we visit much a book is of course kept in which visits and addresses are entered. Beside this, have only a small vase of flowers and maybe a couple of books placed across each other at one corner. These give an air of life even to the smallest hall somehow; and on little touches like these, absurd as it may seem to mention them, depend the artistic completeness of the whole house.

One word more, hats, cloaks and umbrellas must be put out of sight somewhere; while all should recollect that it is extremely easy to over-furnish any place, but especially so to over-furnish a hall, and that in a narrow passage and in small quarters, one had far better have too few impedimenta than too many. The former state of affairs can always be remedied as we come to understand the capabilities of our new abode; the latter can only draw down upon us the objurgations of our friends, the while we collect dirt and dust, and can't comprehend why we are as uncomfortable as we most undoubtedly are.

CHAPTER III

KITCHEN AND BASEMENTS

IF the conquest of the hall be difficult, the siege of the kitchen and servants' quarters generally is one that will carry dread even to the stoutest heart. For as a rule the suburban builder sinks to his lowest depths of villainy here, and either gives a damp and wandering basement wherein no servant will remain more than her month, or a regular cupboard where the stove leaves scarcely room for anything else, and where the heat from that, and the draughts from the doors and windows, are enough to ruin the constitution of any ordinary woman. The basement kitchen is the worst of all, because it marks a class of house that has seen better days, and is rapidly deteriorating. Therefore if one has to choose between two houses, one of which has no basement, and another which has, one should at once select the basementless one. There are sure to be cellars below the house, which will keep it dry. One doesn't even in the suburbs *often* come across a house, the boards of which are pushed out of place by enterprising mushrooms growing in the soil beneath, and ambitious of appearing in fresh air and among the haunts of men.

If, however, the basement cannot be avoided, we must rise to the occasion and do the very best we can in the matter. And first of all we must see that it is really dry, and that its comfort is assured by the presence of a dry area and the proper amount of ventilation, and absence of damp. If this cannot be assured, the house must be given up. Far better put up with a small dining-room and a dull drawing-room, for both of these drawbacks can be easily remedied, but for a damp bad kitchen there can be no cure, and should we weakly give in to it, we can never be happy or comfortable in the least in our domestic arrangements, be very sure of that.

If, however, we find that the basement is capable of amendment, our first endeavours must be to make it as cheerful as possible, and to get as much light and air into it as possible too. I have only once had to 'wrastle' with one on my own account, and that I made as bearable as circumstances would permit, by enlarging a window and having one of Chappius' reflectors so arranged that as much sunshine came in as was obtainable, while I had one of the three doors closed entirely, and made an enormous scullery and washhouse species of abode, into a nice little scullery and a rather decent room in which the maids could sit and have their meals and do their needlework. Oh, I do hope some day to hear of a real and *bona-fide* revolt against the regulation suburban accommodation for the unfortunate maids, for, until this takes place, I am quite sure the servant question will remain a very burning one.

I am writing now more especially for those householders who have from £500 to £1000 a year to spend, and who have two or four maids, according to their means and the size of their families, and who ought to be able to find the kitchen arrangements comprised in a square block, consisting of kitchen, scullery, parlour-maid's pantry, with good, deep cupboards for glass and china, and a pretty little sitting-room where the domestics could have a few at least of the amenities of life. The bedrooms could be above, as could the sanitary arrangements, which are all too often placed either in the cellar part of the house or close to the larder, or, in fact, anywhere where they ought not to be. Now suppose we find the ordinary box of a pantry, slip of a kitchen and scullery and larder, how should we best circumvent this arrangement, I wonder? Well, first we can tackle the landlord, who, if he have money at all: and an impecunious landlord is a deadly and desperate thing to possess, and should be most carefully avoided: will be glad to do as we want for an extra rent at the rate of 5 per cent on whatever outlay he can make. We should get him to build out a servant's sitting-room, and enlarge the pantry and scullery, and to put above the erection a servant's bath and lavatory arrangement. This could be done for about £100 and the extra £5 on the rent would hardly be felt, while the comfort obtained thereby would far and away compensate for the outlay. If the landlord be obdurate, the only thing to do is to buy for ourselves one of Humphreys' moveable iron buildings, and have it adapted for our purposes. In this case we can only, I fear, manage the servants' sitting-room and extra accommodation for glass, china and washing-up, and we shall have to put the room door just apart from the house, though, of course, a very short passage could be erected. But before anything is done, care should be taken to ascertain the rules and regulations respecting the erecting of buildings in the special locality, as all seem to me to differ; and, indeed, in some there are none at all. Yet, in any case this is a thing to be ascertained definitely, for I have known a Local Board step in and formally order the removal of a beautiful and pet conservatory, because the builder had innocently infringed some bye-law in its construction, and had not obtained the sanction of the authorities to the plans of the structure before erection was commenced. If neither the landlord nor Humphreys can come to the rescue, I am going to advocate a step which will be nothing short of anarchy and revolution in the eyes of any old-fashioned person, for I am about to suggest that, in these desperate straits, the usual third room should be handed over to the maids to sit in, while we can keep it in a measure in our own hands too, by erecting our store-cupboards there, and extra shelves for glass and china. But if we do, we must not be always pouncing in and out on the maids, but must give out everything for the day's use before ten o'clock, after which we should never go there unless actually obliged, for nothing is so detestable as a room into which anyone can go at any moment, and where the maids can never feel they are safe from eternal supervision. If the door of this third room opens straight on the hall, and if another can be made to open into the kitchen premises —and this is often the case—it would be well to permanently close the first and have the second made. The original door need be only bolted or locked inside, and covered with a curtain, while it is not either difficult or expensive to contrive another exit, for a hole is easily knocked in an ordinary suburban wall, and a door frame and door added. And I venture to prophesy if this is done, that there will be a reign of peace in the kitchen department unprecedented in the annals of most houses, because servants will usually stay where they are comfortable, and where they feel they are considered, and their health and happiness are both thought about. I know quite well that in their own homes and in the houses they come from, they have no real privacy at all; but I also know that most maids leave such homes at too early an age to recollect half, or, indeed, to realise half, of the miseries they are called upon to bear there, and they very easily forget the past, and only really comprehend the present and its possibilities; besides which, a maid goes away from her home to 'better herself.' Were she content with semi-starvation and over-crowding, she would remain there, or enter on the desperate existence of a factory hand or a home worker. The fact that she wishes for more comfort, for more human surroundings, sends her into domestic service; and if that comfort and those surroundings were forthcoming, servants would be far more plentiful than they are at present, and would likewise come of a far better and much more honourable and pleasant class. The first step then is, undoubtedly, to secure something in the shape of 'the room,' as the servants' hall is called in more ambitious households, and the second is to see that it is decently arranged and is sacred to the maids for a certain portion of the day, and most certainly for all the evening. I say a certain portion of the day, because, in small establishments, it is possible that the mistress may have little jobs of finer cooking, of plate-cleaning, or even dressmaking to do that she cannot well manage in the one sitting-room which would be her portion when the third room is given up to the maids. If this be the case, the establishment will naturally be so small that the maids will be too much occupied all the mornings to be able to use it, so that until 12.30 it could remain in the mistress's possession; but after that hour she must never enter it. Just as in a larger house and with more maids, the hour of ten must see her out of the kitchen, that part of her work being completed then for the rest of the day.

 Almost the first things a housemistress should ascertain about her house are the position and number of the pipes which are part and parcel of the water supply, as, unless this is ascertained, and she is able to possess herself of a species of sketch-map of them, she will not be able to know how to manage should the usual winter arrive in all its strength, and the water become frozen in the pipes in a manner that should never, for one moment even, be allowed. As a rule, our winters are not very long or very severe; if they were we should, no doubt, be readier for them than we are now. But we can always depend on a cold 'snap' or period during which our very unpreparedness lays us open to a thousand and one discomforts and dangers, none of which need have been ours if we had had the common sense to recollect that we should have looked out for and prepared against a state of things that is as inevitable as it is undoubtedly most detestable and disagreeable. The suburban builder, as a rule, has his ideas, and his only, on the subject of pipe laying. One idea is, so to imbed them in the walls of the house that we cannot get at them at all, and another is to place them outside the house in the most exposed position possible, where they are warranted to freeze on the first provocation, unless we can take the matter into our own hands at once, and either box them in, filling in the space between the pipes and the boxes with sawdust, which generally protects them for all time from the severest frost; or, at the approach of winter, so swathe them in flannel rags and hay bands, that frost cannot touch them, not forgetting to treat in a similar manner the pipes in the tank room. These should be our especial care, for they are often the first to freeze, and are the cause of many and many a detestable and untoward catastrophe.

The boiler in the suburban kitchen is generally one of two kinds, and is either of the low-pressure order, which has no system of circulating pipes, or the high-pressure species, which has and which requires more elaborate care than the former. If the low-pressure boiler is the one in use, and the frost is severe, it is better to completely empty all the pipes in the house, and to cut off the water supply to the house entirely, drawing the water from a supply-cock fixed just before the water enters the house, whence it can be obtained by hand as required. Of course this adds a great deal to the work, but it means safety, for when the boiler is kept well filled it cannot burst, neither can pipes freeze if there be no water in them to bring about this very disagreeable state of things. A low-pressure boiler having a lid that comes off, can always be hand-filled easily, while cans of water must be placed wherever one is accustomed to use water freely; and though baths may be curtailed and work increased, no damage or danger can ensue. Therefore the moment a frost sets in, cut off the water from the house, and rely entirely on the hand-filling of the boiler for all domestic purposes.

If the boiler is a high-pressure one, we must be very vigilant from the first moment a frost appears, while we must be ready for it long before it really arrives. The first thing to see is that this boiler is supplied with a safety-valve and a supply-cock; and the second thing to do is to have the principles on which the safety-valve is constructed so explained to us by the man who supplies it, that we shall always be able to ascertain in a moment if it is in working order, or if it is not. For safety-valves are possessed of a demon habit of being out of order when they are least expected to be, and we may be priding ourselves on the fact that we have one, and are therefore quite safe, when the wretched thing may be refusing to work, and we may be on the very brink of the catastrophe we have intended it to avoid for us. Safety-valves differ so very much that it would be impossible to describe here how a house-mistress can ascertain if her own special valve is all right or all wrong. The only thing she can do is to have written instructions from the man who supplies it. These instructions, the plan of the pipes and special rules about what to do in a severe frost, should be in a small book kept among the housekeeping books, and easily get-at-able in case the frost should occur when the mistress was away from home, or if she were ill or in any way unable to attend to it herself. If the supply pipes cannot be got at and protected from the frost as a whole, it is best, once the tanks in the roof are full, to cut off the supply entirely from the main. In this case the local authorities must be communicated with, and the tanks filled by the Local Board by means of a stand-pipe, and great care must be taken both to see the tanks are kept full, and that the pipe between the hot and cold water tanks is kept free from frost. If by any chance the worst comes to the worst, and danger is ahead, the safety-valve will show it by blowing off steam; then out with your fire at once, dear reader; you are done for, and must remain kitchen-fireless until a beneficent thaw sets in.

In the meantime a second stove in the scullery will prevent you from being foodless, and though hot water may be scarce and comfort little, you will at anyrate be safe, and as the maids have their little sitting-room they won't be frozen in the kitchen or thawed in the scullery, as they most undoubtedly would otherwise have been. Of course, if we have our pipes properly protected, and there is no warning from the safety-valve, and water flows freely from the boiler-taps, we are all right. In this case it is best never to allow the kitchen fire to go out, but last thing at night to bank it up with ashes and briquettes, and so ensure its burning without stopping. Of course it should be protected by a guard, and no kindling wood must on any account be placed to dry either in the ovens or on the hot plates by the side. In the morning the fire should be thoroughly raked out, and set going again in the usual way. Unless this is done, the fire will not be good enough for cooking: it will be a caked mass, which will not ensure the cook's manufactures being the success they should be; therefore, in giving our instructions, great stress should be laid on the real necessity that undoubtedly exists for a rebuilding and relighting of the fire for the new day.

Sometimes there are odd lengths of pipes that we cannot protect, and which only supply certain single taps. In this case stop-cocks should be fixed in them in such a way as to prevent the water entering them, and these should be used in the frost. Then these special pipes can be kept waterless without disturbing the whole internal economy of the house as regards the water supply. Of course I am not writing in any measure about the proper arrangements of the water pipes. I am only advising the ordinary suburban residents how to save misfortune, and a ruinous plumbers', and very likely a decorators', bill too, should the winter be as one usually finds it in England, where the spells of frost—undoubtedly short as they are—undoubtedly make people indifferent and happy-go-lucky about their preparations for hard weather.

But given the unexpected in the shape of real cold, and what occurs? Boilers burst and kill and maim people freely, and the moment a thaw comes, the plumbers are besieged by those whose pipes are pouring torrents of water down the walls and the front staircase, while carpets and furniture are spoiled, and everyone's health suffers because the smallest precautions have not been taken to ensure the house against an entirely preventible state of things. Then there is one great thing to recollect, and that is, that after a frost one must flush most lavishly all the drains and sinks, and, moreover, during the frost we must keep ample disinfectants ready and in use in every place where they can possibly be needed. I always put Sanitas down the bath and the housemaid's sink too, because soapy water decays and causes very unpleasant smells, while, of course, Sanitas should be liberally poured down every other place in use. Then when the thaw comes, let the water run freely for at least an hour a day for the first three days down each drain, flushing first with hot water and a liberal supply of disinfectants; for if these precautions are taken, we shall not want the doctor, a gentleman whose visits too often follow a thaw with a regularity far more pleasing to him, maybe, than they can be to us, even if we are as fond of him as people usually manage to become of the family doctor.

I may seem to have dwelt unduly on the great pipe question, but the long frost of the early part of 1895 showed me most emphatically that there was great need to instruct the ordinary householder in the suburbs and in small town houses about this unpoetical but most necessary subject. No less than three boilers burst in one week in the place where I was then staying; one resulted in the death of the servant and total blindness for the only child of the house; one in the death of three children, while the third maimed the cook for life. Of the destruction to property I need say nothing; but when we reflect that all these accidents were absolutely preventable, and were entirely due to crass ignorance on the part of both mistresses and maids, we will, I think, come to the conclusion that the first duty of woman is to know her pipes, the position thereof, and the manner of her water supply; while the second is to be ready to act for the best the moment frost appears, and so render bursting boilers and pipes the impossibilities they both can be made in the most faultily-constructed suburban residences, if only the dwellers therein have their heads screwed on the right way, and are prepared for any real emergency. In any case, it is well always to have some means of cooking, which shall be available should we be, for one cause or the other, unable to use the range, which, by the way, should, if we can in any way afford it, be the 'Eagle,' for at present, at all events, no better one has been invented. If possible, there should be a small open grate and the little side low-pressure boiler which can always be hand-filled; in the scullery or even in the maid's sitting-room; but if either is impossible, we must be possessed of means of cooking by gas, so that we shall not be left entirely helpless should the frost seize on our pipes before we are ready, or should it be necessary to sweep the kitchen chimney or repair the kitchen range.

If, however, we have a gas stove, the supply of gas should not be left to the discretion of the maids, but should only be get-at-able when it is legitimate to use it. Unless the mistress herself can turn on and off the gas, and keep it off when it should not be used, the waste and expense will be enormous. There are certain things 'the very best' maids are always reckless with, *e.g.*, gas, potatoes, bread; and kindling wood and matches; small items to fuss about, no doubt, but small things are what add up and become terrors. One expects the big ones somehow, but the tiny odds and ends, that seem nothing separately, are what swell the weekly bills when they are added up, and therefore should be more thought about than they are in the usual suburban household.

The pipes and the kitchen itself once settled about, the next steps to take are towards proper ventilation and draught exclusion. One cannot ventilate with a draught, yet how few people realise this; if they did, colds would go quite out of fashion and everyone would be much happier than at the present moment. As a rule one door in the orthodox kitchen opens straight on the open air, and here the tradespeople come and linger while waiting about for the orders which should never be called for except under special stress of circumstances. If this be the case, what would it cost to add a simple porch and side-door? not much above £20, yet what a difference would it make in the comfort of the kitchen. If, however, this outlay is impossible, a large, oil-cloth-covered screen should be placed round the door in such a way that one side of it is put by the side of the door which opens, and the door is reached from the other side of the screen, which is only pushed on one side to answer the bell, and replaced as soon as possible. This breaks the draught even if it can't exclude it, while the maids' health and the consumption of coals both considerably benefit by such an arrangement. More Slater's patent draught-excluder should be put round doors and all windows, and ventilation should be secured by a round ventilator put in the top part of the window, and another in the top part of an outer wall; these ventilators can always be closed, but when cooking is in progress or gas is burning, and for at least an hour after the meals are cooked, they should remain open and so ensure that the air in the kitchen should be always pure and fresh.

The larder should be ventilated in the same way, and any windows should be covered with very fine wire-netting on the side they do not open—outside, if they are the ordinary small sash windows, inside, should they push outwards on an iron support—to prevent cats, dogs and small animals of any kind from entering, while great care should be taken to see that the larder is damp-proof. Nothing keeps in a damp larder, and, therefore if it should be damp it is utterly useless to try and put meat, bread and butter there. In any case if one has not tiles, and I never yet met with the suburban larder that had, the walls should be painted from top to bottom, first with Chambers's damp-resisting fluid, and then with a couple of coats of Aspinall's enamel paint in a shade of ivory white. No one should permit the decorator to talk him or her out of using this most invaluable preparation, for nothing I can assure my readers, can take its place. I have had eight years' constant experience of it. I have had many years' experience of the ordinary paint, and I confidently say that it and Aspinall are not to be mentioned together in any shape or form, therefore everyone should insist on its use. The decorator I fancy does not get quite as much profit on it as on the ordinary paint, and it is more trouble to apply I know, and these perhaps are his reasons for his undoubted dislike to it; but if my readers are wise, they will insist on Aspinall, especially where damp has to be considered, and where a good surface and uniform colouring are in request.

The larder should have one wide shelf, and in one corner should be a safe for meat, and poultry, with very fine wire-netting all round. This should be able to be moved and hung out in a shady corner in the garden in the summer if the larder should be warm at all, or else hung in the cellar if there be no garden. Here too should be placed the refrigerator, without which no house is complete, and which soon saves its own cost, in the manner it allows one to keep one's provisions sweet, and one's milk right, and one's butter from running away, as it otherwise does at the smallest amount of heat. The larder floor should be tiled, if not it must be 'gone over' every day with a mop dipped in Sanitas and water to take up the dust and make it fresh and clean; then the food should be nicely arranged for the mistress's visit of inspection, while once a week the larder must be thoroughly scrubbed out, shelf and all, the shelf being washed over with a damp duster daily, when the floor is done over with the ever-useful mop. The same treatment should be given to the scullery, where the sinks should be flushed daily, and which should never be without their big lump of soda in one corner to prevent the grease accumulating.

The kitchen floor should be simply boarded; if only used to cook in, it should have merely one or two large squares of oilcloth or cocoa-nut matting by the stove, kitchen table, or where the cook and kitchen-maid stand to work, and the furniture should resolve itself into a couple of good tables, one the ordinary kitchen table, the other much on the same lines but smaller, and placed close to the window, to be used for pastry making and the finer parts of cooking, and which should both be scrubbed daily, and on which grease should never be allowed to remain for one minute. A couple of ordinary kitchen chairs and the dresser should complete the plenishing. The dresser drawers should be inspected once a week, to see there are no accumulations of rubbish there, and that all is in order. The dresser must never be used as private property by the maids, else will it become a species of glory hole, filled to the brim with unmended stockings, old dusters, paper and string, and odds and ends, which ought not to be tolerated there, or, indeed anywhere else for five minutes by anyone. If the furniture is as severely simple as I have described above, the kitchen resolves itself into what it should undoubtedly be, merely a place to cook in, and in which to prepare the meals. In this case the walls should be painted from ceiling to floor with a shade of electric turquoise enamel, or else in one shade of the blue to about 4 feet from the floor, the rest of the wall being painted a soft shade of brown. This should include the doors and window-sashes, and the one paint should be divided from the other by a wide band of brown stenciling on the blue surface of the wall. The ceiling should be whitewashed, as should be the ceilings in all kitchen premises, and the kitchen should be lighted with a good centre gaslight with a couple of burners. A bracket arm for gas should be on one side of the fire, to use while cooking was going on on very dark days, or when special cooking was going forward; and there should be one gas light in the larder. These lights should be protected with the proper wire-globes sold by most ironmongers. Gas globes are soon smashed in the kitchen, and they are not really safe when they are on moveable brackets or pendants, as they all too often are in these parts of a house.

The pantry should be treated in the same way as the kitchen as regards decoration, and should only have mats on the floor, and no fixed covering there at all. Only the china, glass and silver in use should be kept in this room, the latter, if valuable, only in the day time, and even then in a small locked safe. If the pantry should be large, the extra glass and china can be kept there in locked cupboards, accessible to none but the mistress. Here in the ordinary ship's cabin provided by the suburban builder, the 'fitment' style of cupboard is most useful. As a rule the maid only wants room enough to stand or sit by her sink to wash up and clean the daily silver, and so the tiny space can be almost filled with cupboards; and here is an excellent place for the stores and jam-closet: the ordinary suburban resident if wise, getting in her stores once a week from Shoolbred, and not dealing with the local grocer, who, all too often extracts orders from the maids when none should be forthcoming. If there really is no room here for them, cupboards must be erected in the maid's room, whether it be that vexed third room or another. Somewhere there must be a store-cupboard, properly regulated and properly looked after by the mistress herself, and no one else at all; otherwise, that way most undoubtedly lie bankruptcy and disorganisation, often enough one and the same thing.

The maids' sitting-room should be papered with some pretty, light paper, and should have either a dado of cupboards and shelves in the fitment style, or else a real dado of plain, self-coloured oilcloth, which can be wiped over with a damp duster daily. This and the paint could once more be brown, as could the dado-rail. The ceiling must be whitewashed. There should be a nice table for meals and work, six ordinary Windsor chairs, and a couple of comfortable basket chairs, with hard-wearing, tapestry-covered cushions. These should be considered the property of the elder servants, if four are kept; but, of course, if the housemaid is of 'staid' age, and careful she could have a nice chair too. I think the ordinary kitchen chair a cruel thing, except for use at meals, and see no reason why the maids should be condemned to its use and nothing else, when, surely their backs must ache sometimes as well as the backs of other far less employed women undoubtedly do.

The grate must be a slow-combustion one, and, unless the mistress uses the room need not be lighted, save in very severe weather, before one o'clock, when it should be lighted from the top and allowed to burn slowly down, and kept going with briquettes and small coal judiciously mingled with a little larger coal. The curtains should be of the dark blue and white butterfly cretonne Liberty sells, and which should be in universal use wherever much washing is to be expected, for it washes splendidly, and never seems to wear out. I have still a couple of cretonne covers I had quite thirteen years ago. The floors should either be stained or else covered with plain cork carpet, supplemented with small rugs here and there, or else with a square of cocoa-nut matting. But I like rugs best; they are so easily taken up and shaken, and dust is kept at bay as long as this is done. I am very much inclined to say, do not have gas here, yet I fear unless we have plenty of help we must, or the lamps, inevitable in the sitting-room, will become too numerous for our staff. At the same time, I do very strongly recommend a good duplex lamp from the centre of the ceiling if it can be managed. Servants are reckless of gas. They are not so fond of lighting the lamps as they are of setting a light to the gas. In the first place, it is more trouble; in the second, they know that if they light them too soon they will have to re-trim and re-fill them before the evening is out. But if a lamp is procured, it must be a good one. It must have a metal receiver, and it must have a clear glass shade. Silk or stuff shades are out of place, and very dark always I think; in such a room as this they would be ridiculous, and most likely dangerous. This room is in the care of the kitchen-maid too, though, if there are books, pictures and ornaments, as there should be, the housemaid should take a pride in dusting them and keeping them in order, and should see that the rougher parts of the cleaning are properly performed. As the mistress will use this room for a short while in any case, she can always see that ruin has not begun among the furniture and decorations; for whether it is provided by the builder, or whether she supplement the accommodation of the house herself as advised before, she should always have one store-cupboard here, whence she could give out the things for the day's use. She can then supervise without spying; for once tacitly allow that a room in one's own house cannot be entered save on sufferance (mind, I don't say frequented!) it is easier to storm an enemy's citadel successfully than gain an entry into that special chamber without more friction than anyone who has not tried a similar situation could well believe.

One word more. In frosty weather gas and fires should not be stinted. The gas should be burned steadily in the scullery, pantry and lavatories, to prevent any chance of the water therein freezing. This may save a great deal; but, of course, if the pipes have frozen, one can only accept the situation and wait for a thaw. But that they need never do this, I trust I have demonstrated in a manner that should be patent to the least imaginative housewife in the world.

CHAPTER IV

DINING-ROOMS

THE suburban rooms I myself have personally encountered and conquered have been so truly terrible that, when I look back upon my struggles with them, I can only wonder that I have survived them in the least degree. For not only were they either unduly hideous or over-ornamented in a manner that would strike awe into the boldest soul, but every window and door gaped wide apart, and were with the fireplaces, put just where they ought not to be, while in one or two cases the floors had to be relaid and the doors bodily moved round before the rooms were even habitable. I could only wonder whether the folks who had lived in some of them before (two or three were quite new, and these were, save in one instance, the worst of the lot) had escaped with their lives, or whether they had all gone away crippled in health and in temper, on a voyage of discovery to some better and more suitably-designed, eligible villa residence.

The first room I ever approached with an eye to decoration appeared to be everything it ought to be, and seemed simply perfect. It was large and lofty, had two wide and beautiful windows, and a good, deep fireplace and an excellent floor; but alas! I was not as wise then as I am now, for my only acquaintance with houses was confined to two family houses, in which I had lived all my life, and which were properly built, whatever their other faults might have been: and, in consequence, my sufferings during the first month in that special dining-room were so acute that I have never forgotten one of the numerous pangs and torments I endured: silently, it is true, because then I thought them inevitable, and it is never any use grumbling against things which must be borne! But presently sense awoke in my brain, and I saw that nothing which had caused me such woe need be put up with any longer, and I verily believe the knowledge I have since developed on the score of house-furnishing and decoration first became mine in that special house, for I was roused to the fight with cold and discomfort inseparable from a quiescent residence in a suburban house, and soon discovered cold could be expelled did one rise to the occasion and determine that, somehow or other, one would conquer, and no longer play the ignoramus or the very painful *rôle* of the conquered.

In the first place, the door opened straight on the fireplace, and as the front door—a frail thing of boards and sham stained glass—was about 6 feet away from it, the cold air rushed in the instant it was opened, and the heat of the fire flew mainly up the chimney, insuring that the rest of the room should be more like Siberia than any other spot. And in the second, the windows need not have been glazed at all so little did they keep out the outside atmosphere, notwithstanding the curtains which liberally adorned them, and which used to wave right out into the room at the very smallest approach of a breeze. When there was any amount of real wind, the room wasn't a room any longer, it was one and the same thing as being in the garden, and anyone can easily understand how pleasant it was to come down to breakfast there with a roaring fire going up the chimney and a north or east wind playfully careering around the table, which, place it how we might, could never be in anything save a thorough draught.

The first thing to do was to transpose the door, and make it open with its back to the grate. Then it had to be surrounded with the ever-useful 'Slater's patent'; and, as it opened into the room, a species of shelter was arranged behind it, while a curtain was hung on it—on one of the rods which open and shut with the door—and a pair of curtains put outside it. These hung straight down in good heavy folds when we were alone and there was not very much going in and out; and, as we had a 'hatch' into the kitchen, there never was much; but on 'dinner-party nights' the curtains were tied back, and so did not interfere with the coming and going, as a single undraped curtain always must interfere either more or less. Then attention was turned to the windows, and these were surrounded by more 'Slater's patent,' which was liberally supplemented by putty, because the frames began to shrink away from the glass in a truly hideous manner, and, in consequence, there were two gaps, one there, and one where the frames were supposed to fit into the woodwork round the walls. The woodwork, in its turn, shrank from the brickwork, and the space had to be filled in with mortar and then painted over.

Now this special house was not a regulation £60-a-year villa, but was rented £160, and had a fair garden and good stabling, and was altogether what may be termed a 'residence for a gentleman's family;' nay, even by some house-agents, 'a mansion,' because it had a second staircase; yet such is the material used in the suburbs! I repeat, this special house was a good specimen of the kind, and was not, as might be imagined, a 'fearful example' or an isolated case, so I leave my readers to imagine what the less-expensive buildings can be like, even when they can truly be advertised as possessing tiled hearths, electric bells and all the latest improvements, including a fixed bath, hot and cold water laid on; and other items familiar to those who have gone on heart-breaking journeys in search of a house, liberally supplied with a sheaf of pink and fallacious orders from a house agent. In fact, before the dining-room was livable in, we had to almost reconstruct the windows and doors; and I only regret that my improvements did not then rise to putting in a proper grate, for I am sure, if I had done so, the conquest of the room would have been complete. But unfortunately I did not realise the horrors of it until all the decorations were done and we had settled in, and then expense barred the way; not only the expense of the new grate: that would have been saved in the difference in our winter's consumption of coal: but the cost of replacing the Japanese leather dado, which could not be matched, and, in consequence, would have had to be renewed entirely, because the grate and mantelpiece could not have been moved without spoiling at least a yard of it on each side of the fireplace. A new grate without a new mantel was also impossible, because the moulded mantelpiece, being round above the grate, was not available for the slow-combustion stoves, which are always made square. Everyone should refuse to own a round mantelpiece, because of the impossibility of adapting such a possession to the proper and only really useful grate. If, by the way, Japanese leather paper is used for the dining-room dado, or indeed anywhere for any dado or frieze, an extra piece should always be purchased at the same time, and kept carefully in some dry place, and indeed an extra piece of all wall papers should be secured. Japanese paper particularly can never be matched. I do not think, in all my large experience, I have ever come across a second consignment of a pattern I have seen before; therefore it is easy to see how necessary it is to secure more than one requires at first, else, should an accident occur, or as in my own case, an improvement be contemplated, one either has to leave the accident unrepaired or the improvement undone, because one cannot afford to replace perhaps 24 yards, when a couple at most is all that one really requires.

I have remarked before that in a new house it is absolutely imperative to have large fires going before we begin our decorations, but it is such a necessary thing to do that I must repeat the hint once more, for only after a succession of fires can we see whether the boards and window frames mean to shrink, and if they do we must apply our means of alleviation before we begin to paper and paint. At the same time, we may take it for granted that, try how we may to ascertain them, we shall not find out the real faults and real virtues of a house until we have lived in it, just as we never know our friends really until we have stayed with them or they have stayed with us. But for all that, Slater's patent putty, and curtains will help us immensely, and more especially if we adapt ourselves to the house a little, and realise, for example, that the head of the table can be just where we like to make it, and need not be exactly between the door and window with the fire at the back, because the orthodox dinner-table seems able to stand in no other position.

Now I maintain that no one should ever buy the regulation long dinner-table, and that happiness and comfort, to say nothing of beauty, are much more likely to be found at one that is round or oval than at one that has the usual British head and foot. If it be round, the master of the house sits naturally where his place is put for him, but if not he as naturally gravitates towards the head, regardless of the fact that his back is scorched and he feels ill and uncomfortable, the while his feet and hands are in Siberia, and an icy blast plays about his head because the door opens straight on him, and in consequence he cannot get out of the range of the bitter wind from the passage or hall, try how he may to exclude it from the room. Talk about heredity how one will, and disguise if we dare its dreadful tyranny if we are sufficiently ignorant on the subject to do so with proper complacency, still I venture to remark that the dogma is proved to the hilt every day. An ordinary English family takes possession of the miserable hulks most of our houses are, and settles down without a struggle against them, to patiently endure the preventable miseries inseparable therefrom. There is no real need for any man to sit at the head of a dining-table, generally twice too long, too, for everyday needs. The side would be far more comfortable, far more common-sense in every way, but because the male of the house has always taken his seat in that special position, perhaps at the commencement of the family in a castle the walls of which were 3 feet thick, the present day man does the same and remains there, although he grumbles all the time and 'wishes to goodness' some way might be found by which he could be insured from being starved with cold or fried to death, or indeed often enough both at the same time. Therefore is it well to have a round table, for anywhere there can be the head or the foot, and the man at once accepts the new position, without demur; but given the ordinary table, nothing will move him, argue as we will and demonstrate as we may how infinitely better, in every possible manner, another seat would be for him.

 Of course, if the house be accepted as it is, nothing can ever make it nice, be sure of that. If it be wind and water-tight, and that is a rare experience, the so-called decorations will either be terrible, or else will 'swear' continually at the belongings we bring to put amidst them. Lucky is the woman who finds dirty paint and torn and smudged papers and who does not come across an obstinate landlord and a 'newly-decorated house.' If she does and she possesses an ordinary husband who thinks anything does so long as it is clean and tidy, she should flatly refuse to enter it, for if she has artistic taste her life henceforward will be nothing but misery; for, absurd as it may seem, real pain and discomfort are given by ugly or incongruous belongings; and I venture to state boldly that people would be much happier did they own and realise this fact, and give over priding themselves on 'rising above their surroundings,' a thing no one possessed of the smallest eye for colour or form was ever really able to do. Superior folk always tell us we can, just as they say we ought not to be influenced by the weather, yet 'ought' doesn't come into the matter at all. Maybe we ought not, but then we ought not to be ill or grow old, or be irritable, or anything but severely virtuous and good in every *rôle* we have to play during life, but all these things *are* or *are* not. What they and we *ought* to be or to do is quite another matter, as anyone with a grain of sense will, I think, admit.

DINING-ROOM AT WAYSIDE.

When, therefore, we have duly circumvented the draughts and dangers which await us in the ordinary suburban house, the next thing we have to consider is either how to paint and paper and furnish, or how to decorate to suit the goods we may already possess. If we have already got our furniture, the paint and paper must be bought with an eye to those. Yet as a rule it is so easy to re-cover dining-room furniture that no one should be debarred from having a pretty room because they have ugly seats to their chairs, or own perchance a set of frightful curtains. I am no advocate for cheap materials, which appeal to a 'threepenny public,' and scarcely last until they are made up, such fleeting joys are they: but I unhesitatingly say that, given the choice between ruby velvet and Wallace's old gold diamond serge, or pale blue 'Tanjore cloth' from Shoolbred, the ruby velvet may depart as far as I am concerned, and I should put up the other colour in the cheap material, knowing full well that the beautiful colour would always delight me, while the velvet would disgust me every time that I entered the room. The same remark applies to the carpet. If it be 'handsome,' generally another word for something too hideous for words, put it into the next sale that is handy. Somehow 'handsome carpets,' always fetch splendid prices at sales, where even good furniture is almost given away. Then buy one of the many charming carpets Smee & Cobay, or Wallace, or Hewetson sell, according to taste and means; remembering that all carpets are merely backgrounds to the furniture, and should never attract attention to themselves in any way. One very soon tires of a pattern, an obtrusive pattern that is to say, while one never can tire of soft shades of the same colour, or else of the excellent 'drawing-room' Turkey carpets or Bokhara carpets, sold by Bartholomew & Fletcher and Shoolbred, which suit almost any room, and fit in with any style of decoration. If, in removing to a new house, the mistress has to consider her furniture and curtains and carpet, she must look at them carefully before she begins her instructions to the decorator. Suppose for example she has a big sideboard, ten or twelve walnut or oak chairs, with shabby leather seats, an orthodox table, and perhaps a writing-table, she will, as a rule, come to the end of her impedimenta. Her first endeavour should be to get whoever may be coming into her house to take curtains and carpets at a valuation; her second to put them in a sale; then she can proceed joyfully, spending the proceeds on new ones, which may be much simpler, but will be much more artistic, and so much more satisfactory to live with in every way. If however she has a pretty carpet and curtains, and they will not quite adapt themselves to the room, what is she to do? In the first place if the carpet is too large it is best to return it, if possible, to the shop where it was bought to be re-made into a square, and edged with a nice woollen fringe, if, indeed it was not born square as all carpets should be, and furnished with a good border. The worn parts are thus eliminated but should be carefully kept for mending purposes. In the second place, if it is too small and cannot be matched, it should be surrounded by matting, staining, or plain brown cork carpet according to the state of the boards, and should be supplemented by a large Eastern rug in the windows or by the fire unless the carpet is too small or too frankly British for such treatment. In that case it must be sold or relegated to another room. Unless this is done the result of any manœuvres which may be made with it can only result in abject and total failure. If the carpet be available and be of the new kind of Turkey carpet, it is well to have a good yellow and brown scheme for one's decoration; and, in any case we must have some kind of a dado and that must be sought after very carefully, for sometimes one can come across a real bargain in oak panelling, to be sought for with most chances of success at Hewetson's and at Bartholomew & Fletcher's; while Godfrey Giles' 'goehring' and 'Glastonbury' dados are inexpensive and really good and what they are meant to be. Personally I am devoted still to Japanese leather paper, and these are all the materials I really care about for a dining-room dado, though anaglypta is not to be despised. At the same time it is generally 1s. a yard unpainted and one can get for the same price a good Japanese leather which does not require painting, so there is no reason for choosing the one in preference to the other. A gold and brown leather paper dado should be the first thing to procure, either at Liberty's or Knowles'. Sometimes one has it, sometimes the other; it's all a matter of 'consignments' after all, and knowing where to search for what one requires. Then all the paint everywhere must be 'tea-pot' or 'earth-brown,' while above the dado should be either a vivid yellow paper, an orange, or a soft brown, according to the aspect of the room itself. Orange and yellow look best in a sunless chamber, and a really soft brown, something like the palest shade of chocolate, or the deepest of *café-au-lait*, harmonises best with sunshine that pours into the room from the first thing in the morning until late in the afternoon.

Then attention should be turned to the chairs, and if expense bars them from being re-covered in soft brown leather, and take my word for it, there's 'nothing like leather' where dining-room chairs are concerned, we can either fall back on 'Pantasote,' a species of crocodile-looking material sold by any upholsterer, or we can use stamped and ribbed velveteen from Shoolbred, or Wallace's frisé velvet in golden brown, which will transform the chairs at once, and bring them into harmony with their surroundings, the while new yellow diamond serge curtains are hung, and a diamond serge tablecloth, with a darker velveteen or frisé velvet border laid on is placed on the table. If the awful sideboard must be kept, we must make it as bearable as we can by placing a coarse linen and Greek lace cloth on it which exactly fits the top, and just, and only just, hangs over the edge. We can keep three plants there when the sideboard is not in use at meal-times, but should, as a matter of course, allow nothing whatever in the way of plate and dinner-table accessories to spoil the appearance of the room. Such a room would be quite simple, quite inexpensive, yet always a joy to live in, especially if the rules of plain paint, ivory-coloured cornice and papered ceilings are adhered to here as elsewhere. Trifles these things may be, but on trifles depend success in furnishing, which never can be perfect if the smallest matter is passed over which is not quite what it ought to be merely because it is too 'trivial to matter.'

There are about three different styles of windows in suburban residences, and these are the bow, the ordinary sash, and what I call the '*Randolph Caldecott*' window; and all these can be most successfully treated without using the abominable and expensive roller blind to which Britons are so deeply, so almost irrevocably attached. We have less sunshine than almost any other nation under heaven, yet we of all people cling to the useless and truly ugly window blind with a devotion worthy of a nobler cause. Still I have hopes that constant preaching may do something, and that in time we may realise the fact that nothing but outside blinds are of the smallest use in really hot weather, and that curtains are meant to draw, and that should they fail to be anything save melancholy wisps at the end of an expanse of glass, they are not only useless but absolutely ridiculous in the eyes of any artistic person. The ordinary bow window, if small has been so often written about that I really cannot think it necessary to dwell upon it again; and is it not illustrated not only in *From Kitchen to Garret*, now a respectable classic nine years old, but in Wallace's catalogue, and Smee & Cobay's, and doubtless in others too? But a larger one has not been illustrated that I know of, and while the fundamental lines to go on should be those of the small window, the material curtains should be long, there should be no window-seat in the dining-room—unless there are a couple of windows and no third sitting-room—and the muslin curtains, which are fixed on the window frames and take the place of blinds, should be supplemented by four long muslin curtains, frilled each side, to go under the material curtains in the centre of the bow, and two, frilled one side only, to go one each side at the end of the bow. These curtains should be crossed at the top, and held back high up with wide frilled bands of muslin similar to that used for the curtains. As a rule H. Gorringe's spotted muslin sold ready frilled is the best material for this purpose, but I am very fond of Wallace's 'Guipure vitrage' for the curtains on the window. If this be used, the long curtains should be of Guipure too, taking care to have a double edge to the centre curtains, and a single one to those which go at the end of the bow.

The ordinary sash window, if short, should be treated like the centre window of the small bow window, but if it reaches from floor to ceiling it should have the double set of muslin curtains which I have just been writing about. Then we have only the Caldecott windows to deal with, and these, unless we are much overlooked, should have one set of stout material curtains only. As a rule these windows are divided into two parts, the top filled in with stained glass and immovable, the second plain glass and opening either straight out or straight into the room. The rods for the material curtains should come below the stained glass, and each curtain should be placed to go down the wooden part of the window frame only, and each small curtain should be drawn to keep out the sun as required. If muslin must be had in addition to the material, it must, should the window open out or into the room, be fluted on a couple of rods, which are placed top and bottom of the window itself. But if the window open outwards frilled muslin curtains can be arranged on rods on the window frames, to remain in place whether the window is open or shut, an arrangement which is imperative should neighbours be close, or at anyrate, if we are provided with 'Caldecott' windows in our bedrooms. I do not advise a window-seat unless we have two windows, because no one should ever sit in the dining-room unless it is positively necessary to do so, and, moreover, it is well to use the space for a writing-table and chair in any but a really large house, and that is a place about which I am not writing at this moment. Here can the husband devote some of his time to household matters and letters of friendship when he is at home, while if there is no third room the mistress can use the desk in the day-time, albeit I trust she may have her own in the drawing-room, that is, if she cannot utilise some upstairs room, although under no circumstances can I advise the stuffy and stupid muddle of so-called 'boudoir bedroom.'

Now one word about the curtains which may possibly have to be used, which may be artistic and pretty, and yet may not quite fit the bow windows. If they are too long and wide anyone can tackle them; if they are too short it is easy to make them longer by adding as much holland at the top as is required, and then covering that with an adaptation of Mr Ernest Newton's turned-over draperies. If the original curtain is a plain material, as, indeed, all curtains should be, the holland should be covered by a deep flounce edged with trellis fringe, of some figured material, either a good tapestry or my pet printed velveteen. If the curtain be figured the turn-over drapery should be in plain Bokhara plush or velveteen, while cheap serge curtains can be lengthened by merely joining on more serge at the top, and hiding the join with a narrow piece of ball-fringe merely tacked on. If the curtains are too narrow, they can be widened with a deep flounce or frill of soft Surah silk, or even sateen, in some plain colour, but these devices should only be resorted to if the curtains are really worth saving; if not, it is far better in every way to sell them, or give them away—the ever-ravenous Kilburn establishment is always open to such gifts—and purchase others, which can not only fit the windows, but at once allow us to have, perhaps, far more harmonious surroundings.

Of course, if we are in the heavenly position of having no old furniture, and can set to work with a free hand, and sufficient money to enjoy ourselves, we can at once do just as we like. But no! even then we have to consider the special room and how best to circumvent its idiosyncrasies. As a rule the door is on the same side as the fire-place, or else exactly opposite it, and we may have recesses on each side of the fire-place, or we may have only an expanse of straight wall beyond the door, and not a recess in the whole place. This latter is the worse fate of the two. The recesses can always be filled either with the charming buffets made both by Smee & Cobay, and Wallace, or by colourable copies of the same without backs, made to fit the recesses, which I do not advise, save in cases where money is a great object: then and then only such an arrangement could be allowed. The shelves could be on brackets and the wall behind hidden by little sateen curtains, sateen curtains replacing the doors in the cupboard part. These shelves could

be made by any amateur carpenter and are in any case much better possessions than the dreary, little, badly-made sideboard one finds all too often in far too many suburban residences. These sideboards are machine-made and are cheap and nasty, generally coming to pieces after the first fires have been lighted and always smelling of varnish, and looking more depressing than I can say. If the wall be recessless, and long and hopelessly flat, we should have a good buffet-sideboard in the centre of the wall, in either some good brown wood, or else in my pet stained

green material with copper hinges and fixtures, but with no looking-glass about it anywhere, and with nooks and odd places generally for china and odds-and-ends. Then on one side of the fireplace should be the dinner wagon, as illustrated, made from my ideas by Wallace. The wood can be stained green, and the tray is copper. This is removable, and allows the maid to carry out plates, china, etc. without an effort, thus very greatly simplifying the mysteries known as 'clearing away.' There should be about ten chairs in the ordinary dining-room and these could have stained green frames, and either orange or bright red leather seats. In this case the wallpaper should be real sealing-wax red and cream over a stained green dado, or else real bright orange over the same kind of base to the wall. If money is a great object the seats can be rush, but leather should be managed if possible, and the real orange or bright red are as novel as they are artistic and beautiful with the green furniture. A soft green carpet with very little pattern on, should be chosen, and soft green curtains. The other colour selected should be introduced at the top of the curtain in the turned-over top, which should be of printed velveteen; and if the rush-seated chairs are used, a couple of arm-chairs for the master and mistress should be procured. If there be no third room, leather arm-chairs must be bought and placed one each side of the fire; for here, alas! the husband must smoke if he indulges in that detestable habit, for unless there is a tiny conservatory, and there often is fortunately, even in quite small suburban houses, he will have no other place. But given the conservatory he can smoke there. It can always be made warm and pretty, and his smoking will be good for the plants, and that at anyrate will be some small consolation to him.

Let no one ever persuade suburban residents either to purchase their furniture in a desperate hurry, or to buy what is called modern or Flemish oak, or that most hideous material of all real pale, light oak, which can never be anything save an absolute abomination. As a rule, the modern oak is flimsy to a degree, and is also detestable in design and in manner and style. I would rather have the simplest possible deal furniture, stained brown or green according to my fancy, than either of these materials, which nothing can make bearable in the smallest degree, and I am sure anyone who has had the experience of modern oak I have had—not in my own person, I know better than that; but in the person of others—would never contemplate it for one single moment. If by the way, the hall of the house is blue, it were well to keep the dining-room to the brown and yellow scheme, taking care the draperies in the hall are Wallace's diamond serge, and that the inside *portière* is in yellow printed velveteen, which can be repeated in the turned-over draperies in the curtains. Or we can have orange and cream, having brown wood and orange leather, and a real Eastern carpet with an orange ground which can be found, and therefore must be hunted for, for I have seen them now at Cardinal & Hertford's, now at Bontor's in New Bond Street, now at Hewetson's, and again once more at Liberty's. Know what you want dear readers! and have that and that only, and not the 'next article,' so shall you achieve artistic salvation and in no other way at all; for be sure if one shop does not possess the real thing, another will, and that patience is required in shopping, as well as faith and many other of the cardinal virtues.

But let not the very smallest householder that exists allow herself to have gas in her sitting-rooms on any account at all, neither let her condescend to keep above her head the hideous centre-piece in plaster work which is always provided for house-owners save in the more artistic (and more draughty) houses which have panelled ceilings, the plaster part of which should be coloured cream, and the panels themselves filled in with anaglypta, or else with ordinary ceiling paper judiciously arranged. The plaster rose can be removed in a moment, and replaced by a hook from which a good duplex lamp from Benson & Company in New Bond Street, should be hung, with either a pierced copper or opal glass shade, and this gives light enough for any ordinary occasion; extraordinary ones can have extra light from candles placed on the buffets or sideboard, and in sconces on the mantel and over-mantel, as shown in sketch, the duplex lamp being lighted or not as the mistress likes much or little light, or possesses, as she may possibly possess, branched silver candlesticks, or the equally beautiful Sheffield plated ones which she can place on her table on very grand occasions.

Of course, endless schemes of decoration can be evolved every year, whenever the new papers come out and new materials are produced, but there are certain things which never alter and which should always be recollected. First among them is the fact that we cannot possibly have too much real colour, and that far from demanding the timid compromises so dear to English folk, our climate and atmosphere clamour for real sealing-wax reds, deep oranges, clear yellows, and beautiful blues, and that nothing should make us temporise and have instead the smudgy terra-cottas, crude greens, ghastly lemons, and dull greys and browns which are so liberally provided for us by the usual paper-hanger. Then we must recollect that anything we buy must harmonise with what we have, while, if we have nothing—and happy is she who can begin anew and unhampered by old horrors in the fresh abode—we must buy nothing in a hurry, nothing that does not suit the special place it is meant for. We had better have one good chair than a dozen ugly ones. Also we must recollect that pictures, plants and ornaments are the hallmarks of a home, which cannot exist without them, for these things judiciously chosen and arranged, and not overdone, are after all what turn the worst suburban villa that ever was designed into an artistic abode. But then not one detail must be forgotten, neither the bell handles, the fenders, fire-irons nor finger-plates nor door handles which should be all artistic and all in one material, either beaten iron or copper, or the humbler yet satisfactory plain and untortured brass.

CHAPTER V

PARLOURS

ANYTHING less like a parlour than the drawing-room of an ordinary suburban residence I can hardly imagine; but there is no earthly reason why it should not be turned into a semblance of one especially in those more favoured spots where the architect has artistic leanings, and where the speculative jerry-builder has not had everything his own sweet way. Here we may often come across quite delightful little picture houses, bearing the stamp of Mr Ernest Newton's genius, and if the structure does not equal the design in merit, we can always circumvent any errors if we are clever, while the deep, charming windows and really lovely mantels over-mantels and grates provided for us, make our task of decoration a comparatively easy one from the first. Generally these houses are built with gables, and are half-timbered in a most picturesque manner, and maybe appear at first sight to be over-windowed and unduly ornate, and open vistas before us of swift ruination in the matter of blinds and curtains. But, on reflection, we discover that not only is there not one window too many, but that the very simplicity of the treatment of them as regards the curtaining as described in the last chapter, makes them far less expensive to deal with than the ordinary sash or French window, which one finds awaiting one in the dreadful houses of the older suburbs, or in those which have not yet advanced beyond the tastes of the day before yesterday. Let us therefore contemplate having a pretty room to deal with before we think of the ordinary chamber with its heavy and fearsomely-decorated cornice, its gaping grate, its 'statuary marble' mantelpiece, and its many other drawbacks to decorative happiness. For if we have, as I said before, the task before us is a comparatively easy one, unless of course, we are handicapped by the possession of a ghastly cheffonnier brother in fearfulness to the massive sideboard, a grand piano for a room 15 feet square, or a 'suite' of furniture and a round table, which said possessions really do still exist and have often to be dealt with when a move from one house to another is contemplated. If they have, there is only one word for it, and that is sell. The greater encumbrances must go for whatever they will fetch, and the owners must be contented with a much simpler style of furnishing. The cheffonnier is impossible, the round table may be relegated to the dining-room, and the old-style table there sold: and fortunately these tables are always worth a certain sum in the market: while the grand piano should be exchanged for either a cottage grand or an ordinary upright piano, and the suite of furniture effectively disguised in new cretonne frocks which cover the chairs and sofas entirely, and so hide faulty lines and construction, turning heavy, ugly encumbrances into quite charming possessions at once. These covers, however, must be made very carefully indeed, and must fit easily. The small chairs are finished off with a 3-inch frill from the seat of the chair

DRAWING-ROOM AT WAYSIDE.

not in any case put into a band. A band spoils the look of the frills at once, and gives them a most comic and inconsequent appearance, and the frills on the sofa and big arm-chairs must be arranged on the same lines, though these should of course be very much deeper and should just, and only just, clear the floor. In any case there must be no attempt to adapt old curtains from long windows to these small and artistic ones, for that can never be a success, and materials nowadays are so cheap there can be no necessity for such economy, especially if the house-mistress has the smallest idea of sewing, or knows of a good upholstress, or has daughters who are equal to an emergency. By the way, the very best upholstress I know is Mrs George Bacon, of West Street, Wareham, Dorset. It seems a long way off but it really is not, and she is such an admirable worker and so quick and industrious, that one saves her fare over and over again, and her keep too, as of course save in London, where she has married daughters she can stay with, she has to be put up. But then she has all my patterns, and think of the inestimable value those must be to my numerous friendly readers! Once more then, if we proceed on these lines, all we shall have to consider is the carpet, and we must take the most prominent colour in that, and do our best to live up to it. But on no account must we attempt either to ignore or shirk the fact that there is a prominent colour to be considered. We must make that the key-note, and wall-papers, cretonnes, and curtains must all be chosen with a remembrance of the one thing that we are bound to recollect if we wish for any decorative harmony at all.

When, I wonder, will the dreadful muddled browny-blue-yellow carpets cease to trouble us? When, oh when will the 'magnificent designs' and handsome patterns fade away into the *ewigkeit?* and leave only the charming unobtrusive designs in the same colour, but a shade or two lighter than the ground of the carpet, which are all that should be found in any house in the land? One only wants a warm bit of harmonious colouring on the floor, after all; one does not want the carpet to arise and call aloud to the entering visitor, 'Look at me! See what I cost! Recognise these exquisite touches and tints, these fearsome leaves and flowers, this magnificent and gorgeous pattern which covers me, and renders me so unduly conspicuous.' But rather should it never be noticed at all, thus taking its right place in the harmony of the decorative design, and becoming merely the floor covering that it is undoubtedly only meant to be.

If we are rich, we can have pile; if not, let us have either the three-ply Kidderminster, or the satisfactory 'Dunelm' carpets, recently brought out by Wallace, or one of the carpets kept by Hewetson, Smee & Cobay and Wallace, at my earnest request, where the pattern only shows sufficiently to break up the plain surface. No doubt entire absence of pattern would be the more correct, did that not mean that every atom of fluff, dirt and dust showed at once, and fidgeted the owner all day long. For these atoms seem to accumulate mysteriously the moment any plain-surfaced material is selected, and though I much prefer to see whatever dirt is present, with an eye to getting it removed at the earliest possible moment, one cannot have a room swept and dusted more than once a day, and some rooms cannot be swept as often as that, although undoubtedly they ought to be. Of course my ideal floor covering will always be matting and rugs, and from that I shall never depart. I am devoted to the new 'Isis' matting, sold by the Abingdon Carpet Company, and also to the plain string coloured matting sold by Shoolbred, Treloar, and Liberty at about 2s. 8d. to 2s. 10d. a yard; this, of course, has to be supplemented with rugs, and, therefore, is not as inexpensive as even a good pile carpet: that is to say, if we buy good rugs, and inexpensive ones cannot please, because of the crudity of their colouring and the manner in which they wear. Hewetson's and Liberty's rugs are simply perfect, and can be bought by the tyro in artistic matters without the smallest qualm, for at neither establishment will he or she be given anything which is not just what it ought to be. But given the rugs, it must be once more remembered that there is a certain art in placing them about the floor, which all house-mistresses do not, it seems to me, recognise. The rugs must not be put down in straight lines and close together, but given the ordinary room, should be placed as a rule at right angles to one another. Of course this is merely a hint, and can be improved upon in any way my readers prefer. That such a hint is necessary I know, because I have often gone into a room where there are plenty of beautiful rugs, spoiled entirely by being placed in long lines close together, in a manner that would be painful indeed, were it not utterly absurd. As a rule such a room has one rug straight along in front of the fireplace, another straight in front of the window or windows, while the rest are placed in the same painful positions by the door and by the wall opposite the fire, in a manner which makes me long, no matter where I may be, to oust the furniture on the instant, and to put those rugs myself in the manner in which they should most certainly go. If we must have new curtains, quite the most dainty and charming arrangement can be made from using the new coloured linens, sold by Walpole Brothers, and by Murphy & Orr and Harris & Company. These linen curtains should be full and short, should be double, if there be very much sun, and should have an insertion of Torchon lace laid on about 2 inches from the edge of the curtain where should come a softly-falling frill of similar lace, about 3 or 4 inches wide. These frills should go round the bottom and up each side, and the tops of the curtains should be finished by being slightly gathered on a narrow tape, on which the hooks should be sewn which fasten into eyes on the slight brass rods, which are all that are required in these special windows. The hook-and-eye arrangement is much to be preferred to the old manner of sewing rings on the curtain itself; one can unhook a curtain in a minute and shake it out of doors in another. If one has rings only, it means taking down the rods too and that means trouble, which a lazy housemaid will most surely shirk, if she can in any way manage to do so. By the way, the structural faults dwelt upon in former chapters will most certainly be found in this room, as in all the others, and must be rigorously treated in a similar style, while the *portières* must be placed inside and outside the door, and a screen must not be forgotten. Unless one has a screen the whole of the room is exposed to view the moment the door is opened; we can have no sense of privacy at all while in such a chamber. If the door opens inside to the left, it should be turned round and opened to the right. If this is not done no one can sit by the fire without being almost blown up the chimney, by reason of the draught which will come in at the opening, and make as a matter of course for the unsheltered and gaping grate.

If, once more, the would-be suburban resident enters on her possession of the house entirely free and unshackled by any encumbrances in the way of furniture, and can really set about making such a room as we describe charming; a beautiful parlour can be made by panelling the room for about 7 feet, and having a soft and very pretty paper above. This sounds reckless work in a house that is merely rented, but one can buy panelling sometimes extremely cheaply. Bartholomew & Fletcher have some oak an inch thick, ready to fix, at 1s. 10d. a square foot, while Godfrey Giles's 'goehring' material is cheaper much than that, and can, moreover, be painted any colour preferred. If the oak is chosen, the fireplace should be finished off with a very light and simple mantel in the same material. It must not be carved or unduly ornate, but be quite plain, and distinguished only by its graceful lines. I do not here advise the regulation overmantel, but I should hang above the fireplace the small Chippendale mirror sold by Hewetson for about 27s., supplementing it each side with ring-sconces to hold three candles. The real old ones are very expensive, but very good copies can be had from Oetzmann in the Hampstead Road. Above the oak the paper should be undoubtedly a really good blue. The right blue which is always pleasant to live with, and does not go black at night or a dull grey or any other unpleasant hue, can always be had from Smee & Cobay; and I am also very fond of their gold and blue Japanese leather paper. Still this is expensive, and therefore not to be lightly recommended for it cannot be removed. The panelling can, which is one reason why I speak of what may seem out of the reach of the ordinary suburban resident, who will make his house three times as warm and comfortable if he panels his walls, and will moreover have always something delightful at which to look. The floor should be covered with matting and rugs, and the curtains should be the same blue as the paper, in linen and lace, printed damask and lace, all in plain colours, or else in plain blue linen plush edged fan edging; and the furniture should be simple, graceful and charming. In the bow window we could have a low broad seat or else a writing-table, placed rather across one side of the window. In the centre could be the flower-table, and on the other side we could put a low, corner window-seat, which might be a fixture and part of the panellings. The rest of the room can be furnished as shown in the sketch on page 131, but great care must be taken to have nothing but comfortable chairs and one good deep sofa; and the chairs must not be chosen without due reflection and without being sat in in several attitudes. A really good chair is a possession which lasts one's lifetime, and one that is in the least degree uncomfortable should never be tolerated for one moment. A good reason that for refusing utterly to buy or countenance the detestable and out-of-date suite where none of the chairs are even decent, and where the sofa may be ornate but cannot be a place to rest upon try how we will. If we have this panelled room, we should try and find a Sherraton writing-table at Hewetson's, which has no high back, a thing, by the way, to remember about all writing-tables, which have to stand in a window. The flower-table can be bought at Wallace's, as can the smaller tables and chairs. A sofa and corner cabinet, can be had of Smee, while a 'grandfather' chair is to be had at Hewetson's, and Bartholomew & Fletcher's 'Seabright' armchair must never be forgotten. These are by far the most comfortable chairs in the whole furniture world. If we cannot rise to the oak panelling, a charming parlour may be made from plain 'goehring,' painted some soft colour, either sea-green, electric turquoise or real ivory, and above the panelling should be a paper in the same shade as the paint; if either green or blue is used; and with very little pattern, only enough to break the expanse of plain colour, while if the paint be ivory a dainty floral paper on an ivory ground should be chosen. In this case we should have cretonne covers to our chairs to match the paper, and the curtains could be of the same, or else of my pet invention the plain linen edged with softly falling lace. If we are able to indulge in the panelling, we should have one of the really beautiful anaglypta ceilings kept by Smee & Cobay; or if the ceiling is mapped out into patterns, the moulded parts should be simply coloured cream, and the panels should be filled in with the ivory-coloured anaglypta one buys at about 1s. a yard. I myself never believe in furnishing entirely from one establishment, and think if one does one can never get a real or individual home. It is also much more interesting to develop our own tastes and search about until we find what we want, and not take recklessly whatever Messrs Jones and Smith choose to sell us. If we do, our house will be the house of Jones and Smith, not ours. And is there not one special firm, which shall be nameless, whose taste or want of it rides rough shod over the suburbs, and makes one house the exact counterpart of the one next door; ay, and the one next door to that! Of course, there are many good firms which can rise above the conventional and become individual, and I am thankful to say that their numbers increase and multiply daily. At the same time, a house cannot be really enjoyed or be really our own unless we have ourselves searched and found what we want for it, recollecting all the time that on no account should we spend all our money until we have lived through a winter and summer in it. Otherwise we shall repent as in sackcloth and ashes, because we are sure to discover some terrible need, which we are powerless to supply because we have not the wherewithal to purchase what would make us comparatively if not completely happy.

Hitherto I have been dealing with the house which is out of the common run, and which is pretty to look at, and repays us over and over again for any outlay we may make, the house wherein we are certain to find good grates and simple mantelpieces, and where, though we may not find our special tastes consulted, we may be quite sure that taste and art exist, though neither need be what we actually consider such ourselves.

Alas! and alas again! that I should have to show a darker side of the picture, and one that would most certainly paralyse any unfortunate tenant who has neither money nor an accommodating landlord. But then I say, let no considerations allow anyone to take such a house, for if it be hideous, and the owner is really poor as well as the tenant, nothing can be done for it because there is nothing to spend, and without money all are powerless. An impecunious landlord should never for one moment be allowed to exist. He is a danger to the community. He cannot and will not repair his roof, see to his drains, or keep the outside of his house in order; and though in some places, notably Brighton, the local authorities can give him notice to put his house in order, and should he fail to do so, can proceed to do the work themselves, sending him in the bill and seeing that it is paid; this power is, I fancy, rather the rule than the exception, else should we not see the fearfully insanitary houses we constantly come across, and are as constantly and continually condemning. I go as far as to say that if a landlord cannot cultivate his land, or keep his houses in good order, the State should have full power to buy at once at a regulation price; but I expect that is too Socialistic a move for most people to endorse. Still, I do most unhesitatingly implore my readers, first never to take a house on a repairing lease, and secondly to make sure that the landlord can spend, if he ought, whatever may be necessary to keep the place in really proper repair.

I have suffered from an impecunious landlord, who, while willing to do his utmost, yet really had nothing to spend; therefore I know how disagreeable this state of things can be; more especially if he is, as he generally is, a nice man. Then one can't bear to trouble him, yet why should we replace his tiles and chimney-pots, and sink our money in his drains, or why should we replace his hideous grates with our charming ones, or his worn-out kitchener with our new and superior 'Eagle' range? Yet, if we do not have these things done we are wretched and unhealthy too, and a good landlord is always willing to improve his property, if we are willing to pay him a proportionate interest on whatever capital he may lay out. If we not only find an impecunious but a crusty landlord, all negotiations must be broken off at once and without delay. It is bad enough to have to pay for improving another man's property, it is unbearable to have our improvements called 'dilapidations,' and treated with scorn and contumely. Strange as it may appear, there are men whose ideas of the beautiful include grained panels, heavy and ornate cornices, and the preservation of the plaster excrescence in the very middle of the ceiling. If one finds such a man we can be quite sure he will allow no tamperings with his doors or his beautiful marble mantelpieces, and that we shall have to keep the house as we find it, or incur endless expense and litigation when we leave, as leave we undoubtedly shall,—thus bringing on ourselves the expense and trouble of a move,—because we are prevented from settling comfortably into a house, into which we should never for one moment have been weak enough to have gone. In the suburb where we do not find the pretty houses

I have written of just now, we generally discover the houses to be high and light, and glaringly vulgar and hideous in every way. They have the orthodox three rooms on the ground floor, and have above that, in a couple of stories, from six to eight bedrooms and dressing-rooms and a bathroom, while all the terrible ingenuity of a vulgar mind has been taxed to produce striped paint, heavily moulded and odiously-tinted cornices and vast glaring windows, which drive the artistic woman wild, because she feels almost powerless to cope with them. But she must do it, and at once. She must seek out the landlord himself, flatly refusing to leave matters to the agent; and dealing in these matters direct, must obtain the landlord's written permission to deal with the horrors to the best of her powers. Let us hope that the decorations may not be new and freshly done. In this case the house must not be taken and I am sure that houses would let twice as fast as they do, if when one family leaves, the walls could be stripped and left bare, the woodwork being either left as it is or merely primed for painting. As a rule, no one likes another's taste, and even if the taste be good, it may not suit the next tenant's belongings, neither, should she be about to furnish, may she care to adapt her new possessions to the colours and styles she finds ready for her in the fresh house. Fancy the anguish of being forced to make and inhabit a green drawing-room, after one has longed for years for a yellow one; or pining for a blue hall to find a terra-cotta one one's portion! That it is not ugly is its worst fault, it is only 'inoffensive,' 'unnoticeable,' too clean to touch. A thousand times better had it been hideous, or so black, that questions of hygiene could be raised at once, and the way opened to secure, what everyone should have, an artistic and beautiful home. If the drawing-room cannot be made into a charming parlour, if we must keep the heavy cornice and the frightful mantelpiece, we must e'en do the best we can for the wretched thing. Anyhow we must secure a simple, tiled hearth and surround, and a slow-combustion stove, and we must disguise the mantelpiece by painting it, if we can, to match the rest of the paint in the room, and putting on it the simplest drapery in the world, which is known as the 'Gentlewoman,' after the paper of that name, and which is made by taking a plain strip of material 24 inches wide, and 24 inches longer than the mantelpiece itself. This is trimmed round the sides and front with ball fringe or cord. If cord is used, a bunch of pom-poms should hang from each of the front corners, and the corners are lined on the cross with thin silk or sateen the same colour as the material, and this is simply put on the shelf and drapes itself. It is so simple that people cannot understand its virtues until they have seen it, then they understand at once what a valuable help it is to circumventing the ordinary marble mantelpiece of badly-designed houses. Mind, I am not saying one word against the beautiful old mantelpieces one finds in really splendid and venerable houses; these are often lovely and rightly placed enough. But the usual monstrosity is not like these or to be spoken of in the same book, and can only be treated as I have just described. The tiles of the grate should never be anything save severely plain and of one colour, for anything else is out of place and generally most expensive, and also more frightful than I can say. If the room is glaringly light it must be toned down, and much as I dislike green, it is the only colour one can have. The 'green ash' paper always kept by Smee & Cobay is a delightful colour to live with, and should have paint the same shade of green as the palest in the paper; and one should moreover have some kind of floral frieze with pink in it. I like the 'Magnolia' bought of the same firm, but both Knowles & Haines always keep beautiful floral friezes, and should both be asked to supply or show designs if the 'Magnolia' were not liked, or were out of stock, as might be the case. The frieze-rail from which the pictures should hang from hooks on copper wires, should be coloured the same as the rest of the paint, and should come in an ordinary room about a couple of inches below the top of the door. Now, just one word of explanation in *re* the matter of a frieze, for strange as it may appear, everyone is not yet acquainted with what is meant when the word frieze is used. First of all it is not a border and should never be treated as such; it should never be less than 16 inches wide, and can be as much wider as circumstances will permit, and it should never, under any circumstances whatever, be put on in strips like ordinary wall-paper is, but should be run round the room the length of the roll, not the width. Most floral friezes are so designed that one would imagine such treatment to be impossible, but I have actually known of cases where a 'festoon' frieze, which one would have thought no one ever could possibly make a mistake about, was cut in lengths and hung sideways in snippets, and even then the owner only thought the design 'queer:' She could not see how absolutely idiotic had been the treatment of the unfortunate thing. Then there is another thing to mention: all too often the wry prettiest friezes designed as such, are disfigured with two or three straight lines which suggest to some vague, chaotic and inartistic minds that they replace the most necessary frieze-rail. They do nothing of the kind; a frieze-rail must be had if a frieze is used at all, and I trust that paper-stainers and makers may some day eliminate those lines altogether, and so no longer give a hint that it is possible to do without the real wooden rail. Even on the score of economy those lines are a mistake. One must hang one's pictures from something, and the frieze-rail is cheaper and far more effective than the usual brass picture-rod provided for this purpose. If we have pink in our frieze, we can have a pink or green carpet, or else a dull green one, just flecked with pink, which I think Morris has, or yet again can we have the entirely satisfactory green 'Isis' matting and rugs. I advise the 'Isis' most strongly, for not only is it beautiful and cleanly in itself but it is a home manufacture, and being made from the rushes in the higher Thames, should certainly claim our patronage. If we want a pink carpet, nothing surpasses Wallace's pink 'Iris,' while Smee's soft green carpet, made on purpose to match the 'green ash' paper, is a great success. If the room is very light it is well to keep to the same shade of green as the carpet for curtains and coverings. This does not go black at night, but keeps its colour well. All drawing and dining-room papers and materials should be chosen at night as well as by day, for great may be the disappointment that awaits the woman who only makes her selections in the upholsterer's shop, and by daylight alone. I have seen two materials which are absolutely the same by day become quite contrasts at night; notably in some shades of green, which turn brown in some materials, while in others they retain their colour, and the result can be imagined if this mischance occurs when two materials, such as plush and serge are used together: or when a fringe is used which turns brown at night, on a material which does nothing of the kind! Of course, the windows all through the house should be treated alike, and in all should be the double or single sets of frilled muslin curtains, according to the amount of sunshine which the special window in question admits. Every care must be taken too in all the rooms to keep out draughts, and to let in a certain amount of fresh air, and the rooms must be ventilated in some manner at the top of the wall. In some cases a brick can be removed and the opening covered within wire-netting, the space between being filled with cotton-wool, which is supposed to filter the incoming air; while if possible there should be a moveable ventilator in the windows. Then Tobin's tubes should not be forgotten, albeit the expense of this patent is an item one should not lightly incur. The drawing-room must be lighted by one good duplex lamp in beaten iron or copper, from Benson in New Bond Street, or from Strode, and the wise will have a transparent globe or shade, and will refuse to grope about in the semi-darkness of silken-shaded light. But the amount of further light must be determined by the owners of the room and their pursuits, and may consist of properly weighted Standard lamps: procurable at Benson's, or at Bartholomew & Fletcher's: or by one or two movable lamps placed on steady tables. In any case great care must be taken to ensure perfect safety; a very small table, or one that has no double tray, should never be selected as a lamp-carrier, for if it is, an accident is almost certain to occur. Great care should be taken in selecting the small table-cloths which should be on all tables, and these can be procured at Colbourne's, Godfrey Giles, and the Cavendish House Company Cheltenham, ready to use; and equal care should also be taken to secure proper pictures and ornaments, which must not be overdone in any way; while it is well to recollect that the dreadful 'chair back' is no longer with us, and has been completely ousted by the Liberty frilled pillow, which is as useful as it is undoubtedly beautiful and comfortable.

If we cannot have a new mantelpiece, let nothing induce us to have a regulation overmantel, for never can we procure one which shall in any way harmonise with a marble mantel; so there is no good trying to get one, for we can't. It is best to repeat instead the Chippendale mirrors spoken of before, and equally good to possess oneself of the round glasses with the eagle and ball at the top, which one often is able to pick up in the shops in Great Portland Street along with charming bits of real blue china, if one understands the craft of bargain-hunting, not unless. Under any circumstances nothing but severe simplicity is permissible. A real overmantel, which may be beautiful in itself, will only emphasise the misery below it, in the shape of the mantelpiece, by displaying its evident contrast to what should be a component part thereof; while either the 'Eagle' or the 'Chippendale' has frankly 'no connection with the party next door,' and is existent on its own merits alone, and is therefore all it should be. Now one last word only, and that is about the position of the piano. If it be a cottage grand, it can be placed like the one in the room illustrated. A piece of brocade should be put carelessly on the end of the piano, and kept in place by a few books, and a tall palm should be placed on the table in the bend. No other decoration must be allowed at all. If we have a cottage piano, it is well to put it in one of the recesses by the fire, straight out into the room, and to conceal its hideous back by a simple curtain on a rod, sold by Shoolbred. We should have in a small room a piano stool to hold music, as well as to sit upon, and in the other recess we could place either the grandfather chair or one of the charming courting settees sold by Hewetson. But let me implore my suburban readers, when placing their pianos to do so with a kindly remembrance of their possible neighbours, to select an inside wall in preference to an outside one, and to practise whenever they can with the windows closed and carefully fastened. I have once been near enough to other folks to suffer the tortures of the lost from my neighbour's piano. I cannot, therefore, impress too much upon my readers that a good deal of real pain may be inflicted on one's neighbour simply because the question of the piano has never been duly and properly weighed and considered. I suppose it *is* too much to suggest that no one should play and sing who has neither taste, nor voice, nor knowledge, so I will only content myself with remarking that the farther the piano is placed from one's neighbour the better, and that some consideration on this subject is due from everyone who may possess and will manipulate that which in some hands may be as much an instrument of torture as the wretched barrel-organ itself!

CHAPTER VI

THIRD ROOMS

I HAVE already discussed one manner of disposing of the usual third room, but I hope most devoutly that the unparalleled sacrifice of devoting it to the use of the maids may never be required of anyone. For unless people can sit in their dining-room in the morning; and I cannot imagine anything more distasteful; the drawing-room or parlour must be turned into a regular hack room, and we are deprived at one fell swoop of a nice place in which to receive our guests or of a fresh chamber for use in the evening. It is a great thing to have entirely different surroundings then, and a pretty, well-aired and ventilated room in which to spend the fag end of a day. Circumstances must always govern cases, and there can be no set rules for the universal regulation of all lives, and if English people would only realise this fact, their sojourn here would be made far more interesting than it is at present. No one has ever taken the third room for the maids, therefore no one can ever do so. The door has always been in that position, therefore it must remain so. That room has always been draughty, therefore draughty it shall continue until the end of the chapter. These are the arguments used, if argument of any kind is allowed. As a rule the position is accepted unconditionally, and because an error has been made from the first, it is allowed to continue unchecked when a little forethought would circumvent that special mistake, and would make a room charming, habitable and warm, which hitherto has been nothing of the kind.

Let me illustrate what I mean by an example. At a small house we possess in Watford there is the third room in question, which has been made into a very pretty library by the clever hand of Mr Arthur Smee, but which the first year we were in possession had never been used save as a home for books and a reception place for anyone who might come on business. No one had ever sat there, nor could I discover anyone who would; but I myself was then 'on the shelf,' and had never entered the room at all, being often absent from home, and always, whether there or elsewhere, confined to the circumscribed area of my own bed and sitting-rooms. I had asked questions about the room but could never get a satisfactory reply only the ever-repeated answer, 'Oh, it looks all right, but just you try to sit there, that's all, you'll soon see why we can't do anything of the kind.' Now here is the room produced just as it was before I went into it, and I wonder if anyone can see the real mistake in the design? I own I could not perceive it from the picture. At first I asked if my people were ridiculous enough to fancy the room had a ghost. No not a ghost exactly; but in a tentative tone of voice something quite as uncanny and quite as intangible. Was it draughty? They didn't think so; and yet it was impossible to warm it. In fact, it was quite out of the question that it could be sat in, and there it remained until one day

LIBRARY AT WAYSIDE.

when I felt rather better than usual, and went downstairs determined to conquer or die in the attempt. Dear readers! if you could only have seen that room you would, some of you, never have believed in me again for one single moment. The centre table was heaped with books, old papers and magazines. The matting on the floor had one long, thin and solitary rug. There were aimless cretonne curtains at the window, which couldn't possibly be reached, because the desk was stuck right against it; and, worst fault of all, the door opened on the wrong side, and so whenever it was open the fire was as it were in the passage. And as had been rightly said, there was not a single place to put a chair; and, indeed, the untidy thing in the photograph was the only specimen of the genus that the chamber possessed, if we except an ordinary bedroom seat, and another of a similar kind by the desk, neither of which could be sat upon, save by an individual who had serious writing to do. Then someone had placed in one corner a deck-lounge, in, I suppose, a feeble attempt at being happy, and never did a lounge less deserve its name. It was located between the window and the fire, and therefore succeeded in nothing, save in being entirely out of place and in the way. There too the shelves for books were left as shown in the photograph, and had none of the small curtains over the smaller recesses, so necessary to break up the lines and to serve as hiding-places for old and way-worn literature. The fireplace was hideous, and a Moloch as regards coal, while, of course the room could never be brought above freezing pitch, because of the relative positions of the fireplace, door, and window, each of which was put just exactly where it ought not to be. The design and colour of the room were right enough, but the touches which turn a room into a habitation were never more conspicuous by their absence.

I don't know how it is, but I can put a room straight in five minutes when another person merely grumbles and declares that nothing can be done; and in a pious rage I set to work and very soon had made a considerable alteration in the place. Although, of course, much could not be accomplished until I sent for my factotum Joe, and had the door moved to the other side, that elegant plaster in the ceiling dislodged, and the hideous tiles in the grate renovated. Then I had a good thick *portière* placed inside the door, hung the pictures properly, arranged the books and china, put the curtains where they were required in the bookcase, altered the window-curtains, put the desk on one side, not in the very centre of the window, and imported a couple of deep, good basket-chairs from Heelas, of Reading, and some smaller Liberty chairs and tables. The centre table was put on one side, and not in the middle of the room, with magazines and newspapers; and after that I put down proper and suitable rugs, instead of the big one,—beautiful in itself and in its proper place which was a passage—but ridiculous in the middle of a matted floor, where it resembled nothing so much as a garden walk. Since then the room has been more used than any other sitting-room in the house, and is now pronounced one of the most comfortable in the dreary little place, or, I should say, in what was a dreary little place until it was taken vigorously in hand. Albeit, nothing can make the house a real success, because it is built east and west, and with all the windows to the west and to the north and south: these, by the way, raking the back yards of the neighbours fore and aft: while, except for the bath-room window, there is not one which looks towards the east, where, of course, one gets the pleasantest view and the morning sun: a great consideration in a house which is literally a summer house, and where therefore, the western sun is useless and tormenting. Even in the winter an afternoon sun is no earthly use, for by the time it comes round to the western windows it has to retire ignominiously into a bank of fog or cloud; therefore such a house as this especial one should never be taken unless the owner will close the north and north-west windows, and open out big square bows on the south and south-eastern aspect in the manner the windows should have been placed when the house was built. It is always a pleasing reflection to me that the man who designed this house is dead, and cannot now make any other person as miserable by his awkward vagaries as he has made me. If he had simply consented to one or two alterations, and had given us decent grates, and proper servants' accommodation, the house wouldn't have been 'half bad,' and I do not suppose would have cost a farthing more to build than it cost at first. The cornices were so terrible that they had in some cases to be cut away and reduced to one-fourth, while the elaborate and expensive style in which they had been liberally picked out in all the colours of the rainbow, was obliterated by colour-wash at once; yet the money spent on this 'decoration' would have gone some way towards new grates; and my pet plain wooden mantels would not have cost half what the monstrous marble ones did, with which one can't wrestle, because of the round openings in the mantelpieces, which would not allow of the cheap introduction of the pretty, square, slow-combustion stoves, with plain tiles, to which I must confess I am absolutely devoted. I think, if their third room in any way resembles the one illustrated here, this picture will help my readers very much, if they are anxious to have a library, a room where the master can sit and smoke, and where business people can be interviewed. But, if books are not plentiful, and the husband doesn't smoke and is not much at home, the room would not be of very much service to the mistress and her girls, should she be fortunate enough to be the proud possessor of grown-up daughters. And there are, of course, yet other means of treating and disposing of the room. If children are numerous, and bedrooms few, this third room may have to be taken for schoolroom purposes, or, at best, may have to be used by boys and girls in the holidays, or when lessons have to be prepared, and in this case it would require quite different treatment to what it would receive were it merely a pretty sitting-room, as it should most undoubtedly be.

If the sitting-room aspect has to be considered it should be made as bright and charming as possible, and should be furnished with an eye to the particular occupation of the house mistress, who is sure to have some idiosyncrasy, and will either work, write or 'housekeep' indefatigably. If she does this latter, she will want room for her household books, her receipt books, and her house books, containing all kinds of hints as to what to do and when to do it, which any woman collects if she is in the least house-proud and anxious to make the most of her surroundings. In this case, one of the recesses could be fitted with shelves on the same principle as those shown in the photograph, but they should not be higher than the mantelpiece, and where there is a gaping space, curtains should be hung, or else doors placed to make a species of cupboard with copper hinges and a good lock. In the other recess a writing-table could be placed, with some shelves above it to hold books of reference, and this table must be furnished with really good locks, for here should be kept account and cheque books, and receipts and any private unanswered letters. Though let me once more impress on all my readers never to keep any save business letters, and never to keep those when the business to which they refer is completely done with and ended. No one knows how long he or she may live, nor if sudden death or illness may not leave all one's secrets, should one have any, or the secrets of others, open to anyone who may have access to one's belongings; besides, we have no right to keep other folk's letters, once they are replied to. We may ourselves be secrecy itself, but we cannot answer for the secret-keeping capacity of our nearest and dearest.

If the window should be, as I hope it may be, one of the delightful Caldecott ones, it should have a straight window-seat arranged exactly as in this sketch, and thus we should be provided with a most comfortable place to rest in, more especially if we supplement it with several big Liberty pillows. These can be covered in plain linen covers, edged with frills of the same or of Torchon lace. If this latter be used, a wide insertion should be laid on all round the pillows, about an inch from where the lace is sewn on. The lace must not be too full. If the pillow should be a yard square, or the more ordinary size of three-quarters of a yard, the quantity of lace used should be one-half longer than the length of the sides of the pillow, *i.e.*, 6 yards of lace would be wanted for a pillow the sides of which measured 4 yards, while 3 yards would be sufficient for the smaller size, as the lace is only just fulled on. It should not be heavily gathered, or it will not look well.

Beautiful pillows can be made by Miss Goodban, of 9 Westbourne Terrace Road, Hyde Park of these same linens. She embroiders them all over in flax and edges them with Torchon, and if these cases are simply buttoned on like an ordinary pillowcase they can be washed in an hour and replaced. Liberty silk covers also wash splendidly if one has a careful maid. I have never sent mine to the ordinary wash; but washed at home they came out of the trial as good as new; a fact I do not think many people can know, or we should not see as many dirty covers as we do in the houses of folks who ought to know a great deal better. The window-seat cover should be of some hard-wearing material, such as ribbed and stamped Victoria cord, or a really good all-wool tapestry. It is never the least use to use one of the cheap tapestries provided so lavishly nowadays for this purpose, for if we do, we shall at once be terribly disappointed by the effect. For these seats in most rooms have a great deal of wear and in consequence if a cheap stuff is used it will not last any time. To ensure real and satisfactory length of days for any material, we must have one made of all wool, and not wool and cotton mixed. The actual expense of these seats, and indeed of any fitted seat, is the upholstress's time and work, which costs as much if the material is only 1s. a yard, as it does if one pays a guinea for the same amount, besides which there is the continual worry of the British workman amongst us. Though why women should not be their own upholstresses I for one can't think, and I should strongly advise any girl about to marry on limited means to learn to make up her own covers and cushions as well as how to cook the dinner. Then if the husband has a knowledge of carpentering and is handy about the house, the place can always look nice at one-third the expense it would cost were a workman or workwoman sent for when the smallest alterations were required.

Given the window-seat there should be no need for a sofa, and that is a decided consideration, but whatever chairs are had they should be comfortable ones, and none are better than the excellent wicker ones of which I have so often spoken. If expense be a great object one can frequently buy these chairs from travelling hawkers who go about the country with vans of chairs tables and baskets, and sell these special chairs for about 5s. or 6s. in wicker, simply stained a faint brown, which said staining I much prefer to paint or enamel, as it never becomes in the least shabby. A cushion must be made to fit the seat finished off with a 4 or 5 inch frill, not any deeper, and another cushion must be made to fit the back, while another must be placed round the sides of the chair, properly stuffed and 'buttoned down.' This said buttoning down can be done by an amateur if she purchases the proper needles for the purpose and secures the buttons with very strong packthread. And I consider such cushions should all be made in this style, as a plain surface wears out twice as soon as one that is arranged with buttons; while, if one is clean and careful, the buttons need not mean an accumulation of dust and dirt, both being got rid of perfectly well if the cushions are properly brushed and beaten and attended to by a housemaid who knows her work. By the way, it takes $2\frac{1}{4}$ yards of double-width material to make a cover for an ordinary wicker chair, or $4\frac{1}{2}$ of single width material or of cretonne, but I cannot advise cretonne for the purpose, or for any real hard wear on any chairs, it so very soon becomes dirty, and is always in the wash-tub and in the hands of the upholstress. If the room is very tiny the window-seat can be furnished with three deep drawers in which we can keep any amount of odds and ends. Of course, the number of the drawers will depend on the length of the window-seat, but three should be the outside number. In any case they would come just under the seat and be hidden from observation either by the deep frill or a woollen fringe, and should open and shut very easily indeed. In a small house these drawers would be invaluable for one of the principal drawbacks to a suburban residence is the fact that there are no cupboards in them, neither are there many recesses which we can utilise as wardrobes should we require to do so. Let us suppose that this special room is given over to the mistress of the house and that she is content to have the ever-delightful shade of 'Panton' blue, than which nothing is better in every way to live with, she would then have the short curtains shown in the picture of some yellow material, Wallace's diamond serge for choice, lined with sateen or plain serge, if there be many draughts or very much sun: then the material for the window-seat should be in golden brown or turquoise blue stamped Victoria cord, and the cushions should be in yellow, blue and pink linen, worked in very coarse and thick real flax by Miss Goodban. If the room has very much traffic, the floor should have a surround of plain brown cork carpet, with a good blue square of Wallace's Dunelm carpet in the centre, just lightly fastened down in such a manner that it can be easily removed for shaking. Personally, I never like nails put in any carpet; they cannot help spoiling and tearing it, and it is far better to sew on the carpet itself a succession of tiny bits of tape, of course on the wrong side, and close to the edge. In these pieces of tape should the nails be placed. The tapes can always be renewed, and in this case the edge of the carpet is never touched, and cannot present the 'worried' appearance which characterises so many really good floor coverings. In this special room the carpet should be in a special shade of blue, which would harmonise with the paper. There are two or three different ways of treating the walls of such a room, and the one I prefer is to have electric turquoise Aspinall for all the paint, the Panton blue paper, and a floral frieze with a great deal of yellow in it; or, again, one can have the blue paper, but with real ivory paint, and an anaglypta dado painted in the same shade instead of the frieze; while a really useful and hard-wearing room may have a soft brown dado, and all soft brown paint, and a darker blue paper. In this case both paper and paint must be selected by someone who understands the science of colour. The brown should have a good deal of cream in it, and the blue should have a great deal of indigo and not any shade of green or turquoise at all. Here the window-seat cushion should be covered in brown stamped Victoria cord, and the curtains should be in blue serge or Tanjore cloth. I have never yet found a blue serge which would stand sun, and not fade in a couple of weeks in the most distressing manner, while almost any yellow serge stands the sunshine, and I can myself guarantee Wallace's diamond serge in yellow, for that has proved itself absolutely fast. Shoolbred guarantees the Tanjore cloth, but personally I have had no experience of this material, having had neither opportunity nor occasion to try it. It is 4s. 9d. a yard, and is very pretty to look at; and is besides a most excellent width. Need I say that any cornice in this room must be simply coloured cream, and the ceiling papered in some inexpensive and pretty yellow and white paper? If blue should be objected to, or one is tired of it, a very pretty sitting-room can be made from any floral paper which is really good, and, *I* say, hand-made. I am devoted to a beautiful heliotrope and green clematis paper sold by Smee & Cobay, and also to the 'ragged robin' paper sold by Haines, and either of these papers should be used above a dado of some kind or other. A full green sateen curtain dado is the best, and in this case all the paint should be the same shade of green as that chosen for the dado, and that should be one of the tints in the leaves on the paper itself. Then the carpet and curtains should be green, and so should be the window-seat and the ceiling paper. The other shades in the paper should appear in the cushions and table-covers: although as regards the clematis paper I have never come across any good heliotrope materials, and have only found this colour in silk and in a capital cretonne sold by the Cavendish House Company, Cheltenham. I fancy that Warings, of Liverpool, have also a good 'lilac' cretonne. They certainly possess an admirable wall-paper with lilacs on a striped background, which should not be forgotten by anyone who thinks of using that always satisfactory decorative harmony of heliotrope and green. If there is not much wear in these rooms, I should advise the green 'Isis' matting as a background for rugs, but if there be a great deal of traffic, the soft green 'Roman carpet' sold by Shoolbred does excellently with some sort of a 'surround' which is easily cleaned, such as Jackson's varnish stains, or plain cream matting, or plain cork carpet, according to the state of the floor and the particular tastes of the owner of the room, who should of course have one of Giles's removable parqueterie surrounds if she can afford it. In any case she must never allow either a fitted carpet or a patterned surround to fidget the eye, avoiding as a real sin against the first principles of art, those terrible materials which imitate parqueterie or tiles, or pretend to be anything save what they are, and giving a wide berth to felt, an admirable material to look at, but a fearful and abominable dust-trap. So indeed are fluffy materials of any sort or kind if they cannot be cleaned without sweeping or by the friendly aid of a damp duster, which just passed over them once a day, keeps the stain or matting or cork carpet in order, and prevents the accumulation in corners that must ensue if we have not a washable material as a surround to whatever carpet we may select. If we have matting all over the floor, it is well to recollect that salt and water form an excellent mixture to use to cleanse it with, the salt in some way preserving and toughening the fibres of the matting as well as cleaning it in a most effectual style.

The principal things to recollect in this, and, indeed in any room are, first, that it must be made draught-proof and be properly ventilated, that we must so arrange that the door does not open right on the fire, that while the furniture may be as simple as we like, everything must be made to harmonise, being either bought for or adapted to the room itself and the special occupations of the room's mistress. Fortunately if our purses are light, there is abundance of inexpensive furniture in these days which I cannot, I feel, praise too highly. I remember the dreadful struggles I had, to make my own first house pretty some six-and-twenty years ago, when there was nothing to be had but heavy wood and solid repps, and no one had whispered 'Liberty,' or mentioned serge, or bamboo and wicker furniture, or, if they had, had murmured it so gently that the murmur had not reached the ears of anyone at all. Now, scoff as one may at wicker work and bamboo, I venture to say that by them lies the way of salvation for the third room in an impecunious household. I have bought the most charming and beautiful little cupboard tables at Shoolbred's, the most comfortable and excellent chairs at Smee & Cobay's, at Heelas, of Reading, and at Wallace's, which have all the delights of a real upholstered expensive arm-chair, if one has the cushions made at home, at as many shillings as the other costs pounds. While the most useful bookcase I ever came across is also matting and bamboo, and this can have a species of cupboard shelf made by hanging a curtain over the third receptacle for books, which said curtain is like charity: it covers a multitude of sins in the shape of rolls of wall paper, odds and ends of patterns, and old books which have seen better days, and yet are not good enough to re-bind, and yet are too good to throw away. Indeed, no book should ever be treated in such an ignominious fashion. At the worst it can be sent to a hospital, or be kept in our own special hospital box, which should be in every house, for how can we tell when infectious disease may not find us out? In that case we shall be thankful to be possessed of something to read which we can afterwards burn without any *arrière pensée* in the matter at all.

One thing should be in every morning-room, or third room, or library, call this little chamber by what name we will; and that is an invaluable small closing-table I have discovered in Kensington High Street. It costs about 4s. 11d., simply stained dark brown, can be folded up and put against a wall, or laid under a sofa when not in use, and is altogether most unobtrusive and excellent, for it can be set up in one second, and is admirable for a thousand purposes. I think it is large enough to 'cut out' upon, although I am not an authority on the subject of work. I know it is extremely handy for tea, and that one can make scrapbooks upon it, and write upon it too, while as it can be folded and put on one side at any moment, it does not get over-crowded with books and ornaments, and is therefore always available. The ordinary small occasional table never can be that, for it is usually clad in a nice square table-cover and has flowers or a plant in the centre, and has moreover, every available corner filled with books and 'twos and threes,' while the modest and retiring folding-table only comes out for use, and is never ornamental, and will not be used otherwise than for the purpose for which it is made. Of course the walnut Sutherland table is much nicer in every way, but is not to be had under 30s., is often of most inferior wood liable to scratches and spots, and is also all too often opened out clad in its tablecloth and ornamented to death. But we have no qualms about the little cheap folding-table. If it is scratched and spotted it can be scrubbed clean and given a new coat of Jackson's varnish stain and be in a moment as good as new if not better. Just one word *en parenthèse*, as it were, about stains. Do not let anything anyone can say induce you to attempt the beautiful green staining we all so much admire at home, for if you do, it can be nothing but a most ghastly failure. True, the particular piece of furniture will be green, but such a green! for the proper effect can only be obtained in the same way really good French polish is procured, and that, as everyone knows, can never be got save by a professional hand who knows the work, and has never yet been known to divulge the secret of success. No; the green stain is not for the amateur, be sure of that, while the 'oak,' and 'dark oak,' and 'walnut' varnish stains are exactly all that they ought to be.

In this room a screen by the door is often a most blessed possession, and as screens can be bought so cheaply nowadays everyone can avail herself of the comfort procured by a judicious use of them. Liberty first, and Shoolbred next, should be searched for an inexpensive screen, for sometimes Liberty has none, and then Shoolbred may come to the rescue, or our experience of both shops may be reversed; it all depends on which place has had the last consignment from Japan. I bought a beautiful screen at Liberty's one year, about a month before Christmas, for 18s. 9d., but on applying for another in the following March, found all were sold out, and I had to go farther afield, discovering the one I wanted in a shop in High Street, Kensington, the name of which I have forgotten. True both Liberty and Shoolbred had plenty of screens but neither had an inexpensive one, with a back warranted to resist the frequent and uncalled-for assaults of the British housemaid. By the way, a screen should always be placed behind the door, which should in most cases open from left to right into a room if the room is in the least degree like the one illustrated. I am not fond of a door opening into a hall, and of course the perfect door should not open, but slide into the wall, but perfection is a word never heard, and certainly not understood at all in the usual suburb.

If the room be blue, the *portière* should be of printed velveteen in shades of yellow. With a floral paper it may be pink or green, but in any case a plain material should not be employed as a *portière*. One should always have a figured stuff there, and if one can afford it one cannot improve on the aforesaid velveteen. *Portières* should be made up by a really competent hand and should be lined, and edged with either 'grip-cord' or fan-edging, as ball fringe is apt to come to grief in this situation, the *portière* being often caught in the door, or as often grasped either by the parlour-maid as she announces a visitor or by any small child who may have to open or close the door. I may seem to speak unduly on the subject both of *portières* and screens but unless they are employed freely, I can assure my readers they will never circumvent the ordinary suburban residence, but that if both are used, any house, even the most jerry-built one which ever disgraced a 'Park,' or blotted the erst-while fair appearance of a 'Grove,' can be made habitable. Without these aids to health, to say nothing of decoration, such a house would be an impossible home for anyone not born and bred in the Arctic regions; while outside blinds, if they can only be just nailed up *pro tem.*, and be mere grass mats bought for a few shillings at Treloar's, can circumvent extreme heat, which often is as bad to bear in these terrible houses as the excessive cold and draughts which characterise them. I know that as a rule three years sets the suburban tenant on the prowl, and, as I said before, the mere idea that such can be the case prevents many a woman from making her house either pretty to look at or even weather-tight. But three years' experience of untoward weather in a jerry-built structure can undermine the health of any woman, whereas she probably would not move and would certainly keep much better in health if not entirely well, did she do her utmost to get over the drawbacks at once. At the same time the hall must be warmed by using the small, portable stove sold by Wolff & Sons, 119 New Bond Street, if it is out of the question to obtain warmth from a real fire-place, and very great care must be given to ventilation by wide-open windows whenever it is possible, and it is always possible during some part of the day: and by ventilators, as suggested before, which should always be open at night, especially when lamps are lighted and fires kept up. For an unventilated room means a sleepy head, and dulness and stupidity instead of the liveliness which should characterise a gathering of the family when the work of the day is safely over and done.

CHAPTER VII

THE NURSERIES

WELL may the heart of the ordinary mother of a family sink within her shoes when she sees the regulation rooms provided for the use of the children! Nay, one can hardly believe that they are meant for them at all, for nowhere are two rooms placed in such a manner as to make real day and night nurseries, and she is lucky indeed who has not to place one room on the first, and the other on the second floor, thus making it impossible for the nurse to look after the children or their garments in the manner she would be able to do were both rooms on the same storey. But it is always possible to have them on the same storey if convention is defied, and the 'spare room' is relegated to the attics, or the nurseries themselves are placed there; and moreover no considerations of any 'spare room' should prevent there being a couple of nurseries in any house. It is odious never to be able to entertain one's friends even for the usual Saturday to Monday visit so dear to the heart of the ordinary suburban resident; but it is far worse to keep the children in one room only, alike for day and night use, and I sincerely hope that this unhealthy and disagreeable practice may soon cease entirely to exist. If in a tiny house and with one baby only, a second room cannot possibly be had, the only way to arrange matters is to proceed on the lines of a Harrow boy's room, and to have either a system of 'fitments,' or to shut all the washing and dressing apparatus into a cupboard sort of arrangement, and to have one of the small folding iron beds, with a wire mattress complete, which cost about 16s. 6d., and which can be put under another bed in another room during the daytime, the mattress and other bedding being folded up and disposed of in a similar way. Yet in such a wee house as this, the baby would usually be in the mother's room, and the nurse could share a room with another maid, having her meals in the servants' sitting-room or the kitchen, while the mother herself looked after the infant. But I fancy where this would be the case, decoration would not be a study, all the energies of the mistress being spent, and very properly too, on making both ends of the income meet if that be possible. At the same time, I can never see why a cottage need not be pretty and comfortable, and I hope that no one will be debarred from attempting to possess a pretty house because she is poor. Pretty things are nowadays as cheap, nay often cheaper, than ugly ones, and it only requires common-sense and the possession of a certain amount of taste to ensure that a house shall be both artistic and comfortable. Let us take first the unfortunate who really can only have one nursery, and who has to allow the child to sleep there at night with the nurse, for I always think it is unwise for the parents to have an infant in their bedroom even when it is very small. A man's rest broken, means bad work during the day, while a woman is unfit for anything and certainly cannot do her work if she has had no sleep during the orthodox hours of repose. In this case the best room in the upper part of the house should be taken for the nursery; it should be as near the mother's room as possible, and if there be a dressing-room attached, so much the better in every way, for out of that can be constructed the very necessary nursery pantry. Therein can be kept everything which is in any way unsightly, and it is possible that all signs of the nursery itself being used for a double purpose can be concealed, if one has at one's service just an ordinary bedroom and dressing-room. We will therefore suppose that, in the first place, the suburban villa contains a bed and a dressing-room, and another bedroom and a bathroom on the same floor. In this case, I should propose that the so-called 'best room,' with the dressing-room, should be given over to the nurse and child, the master of the house having the bathroom entirely for his own use as dressing-room. If this arrangement is made, the bedroom which I trust may face south or south-east, can be treated entirely as a day-room, and be properly and prettily painted and papered. Under no circumstances should one of those fearsome 'nursery' papers be allowed, neither must a cheap and vulgar flower paper be

COMBINED DAY AND NIGHT NURSERY.

used. If expense is a great object, and it would be probably in such a wee establishment, an inexpensive, geometrical-patterned paper must be chosen, with as little real pattern on it as is possible, great attention being given to the colour; which after all is the principal thing to think about in all decoration. For such papers, one cannot improve on the 'Olive Leaf' papers, sold always by Godfrey Giles; and though these special colourings have been obtainable for quite ten years, I have never found anything which would quite take their place. They are 9d. and 1s. 6d. a piece. I advise the latter, the extra 9d. quite doubling the time that the paper will really wear. Some of Liberty's damasque papers are also most suitable for these and, indeed, for any rooms; but these are 2s., and, in consequence, would cost more to put up. Lower than 1s. 6d. I cannot think it is wise to go, for after all, the great expense of papering is the labour, and the vagaries of the British workman render it undesirable that we shall have to employ him more than we can possibly help. For, once he is in the house, heaven only knows when he will leave; and while he is there, everything is disorganised, the maids being engrossed by him and his doings and his followers, and nothing going on in its accustomed and regular routine. I am very fond of the soft apricot shade in the damasque papers, and should often advise one of these used with either real ivory or *café-au-lait* paint. At first, one need not put a dado, especially if the room be prepared for 'number one,' as that can always be added later on, when the room begins to look a little shabby round the base of the wall. Then if the master knows how to use his hands at all, he can simply screw on a dado rail, made of the ever-useful 'goehring,' while the mistress can make a full curtain dado of some inexpensive blue and cream cretonne. Oetzmann often has one at about 5¾d. a yard. This is easily made up, a very deep flounce is manufactured, and a yard and a half of cretonne suffice for a yard of dado. It should be slightly gathered on a tape, and the width of the cretonne makes the depth of the dado. On the tape are sewn very small rings, and these are passed over brass-headed nails put close under the dado-rail, which should be painted after it is fixed, the heads of the screws being covered with putty also painted over; this effectually conceals all traces of them. It is easy for anyone to calculate the cost of such a dado exactly; but, as I said before it can always be added to a room, should it not be advisable on the score of expense to put it up at first. If the soft apricot paper is selected and the room is a very sunny one, I should advise blue Bolton sheeting curtains from Burnett, made double and edged with grip cord, as most undoubtedly anything in such a room should be capable of being washed, while a square blue 'Dunelm' carpet should be laid in the centre of the floor, the outer space being covered with plain brown cork carpet. On no account should a nursery be covered with linoleum, oilcloth or cork carpet; a real woollen carpet should be *de rigueur*. Nothing is worse for a child to creep on than the cold surface of any material which resembles oilcloth, while it is the fault of the nurse entirely should a carpet be spoiled in any way. So, should the mother find the carpet becoming the worse for unfair treatment during the first eighteen months of a child's life, she must realise that her nurse is to blame, and that a woman who permits such 'accidents' is unfit for her position, and should take some situation where the spotless carefulness and cleanliness which should mark anyone who has the care of a child are not required. For be well assured, if a nurse be careless and untidy in one way she will have these same failings in all she has to do. A nurse may herself look the picture of all she ought to be, but if her rooms bear the least signs of neglect, if the child is not 'turned out' like a new pin, and has not perfect 'manners' by the time it is a year old, she must go. Unless she does, there will never be peace in the nursery, neither will the children ever be well. People may feel inclined to scoff at the notion that a child's health can depend on its appearance; but this is a fact, and no amount of scoffing will alter it. If, for example, you see a child sent out with untidy boots, coarse stockings in which there may be a hole or two, and which said stockings are not pulled up trimly and correctly under the short skirts or the neat little knickerbockers; if the under-garments are showing either at waist or knee, if the clothes are unbrushed and awry and the hair unkempt, send the nurse away at once. If she be careless about the looks of the children she will be careless about their health. Her rooms will be either stuffy or draughty; she will not discriminate about the children's food or their times of sleep or play; she will not see the boots are repaired and the clothes aired; she is utterly untrustworthy.

I have had a large experience of people of all kinds, and I can honestly say I have never found a sloven a good servant, or an untidy woman one who could be trusted in any position in one's household. Bad as this fault is in anyone, it is desperate indeed where children are concerned, and should therefore never be endured for a moment. The nurse who is really fit for her post takes as much pride in the children's appearance as the mother does herself. Should she not do so, colds are incessant, and small illnesses frequent, while should there be an infant matters are still worse, for the baby's bottles are sure to be badly kept; indeed a child may die, or at the least may suffer severely because of the untidy habits and slovenly ways of the nurse. One of the easiest ways to discover what manner of woman she is, is this very question of the carpet. And should she object to one and suggest oilcloth, be quite sure she does not know her business, or only wants to save herself trouble. A carpet is a necessity in a properly-managed nursery, and that should be an axiom which should never for one instant be forgotten.

I should never paper the ceiling of a nursery, neither should gas be allowed there; neither should we overcrowd this room with furniture, nor should we permit a vast accumulation of toys. The ceiling should be washed cream-colour once a year, and the room, if small, should be lighted with a good duplex lamp from the centre of the ceiling; also from one swung out on an arm near the fireplace, if the room be large and the nurse wish to sit near the fire to do her work, or wash and undress the children there in winter. No lamps should be allowed to stand about anywhere and all must be out of the reach of the children, else will accidents certainly occur. The lamp must be re-trimmed and refilled daily downstairs by whoever attends to the sitting-room lamps, and must have a metal receiver. It must also be the reverse of cheap. Cheap lamps are dangerous and abominable in every way. Yet a lamp must we have in our nurseries if we wish the children to be well, and to escape the blighting influence of a gas-vitiated atmosphere. If no maid can be trusted to do the lamps the mistress must see to them herself. She need not take more than half an hour about the three or four which would be all that were used in a small house and she will reap the benefit in the children's health, and in feeling confident that the lamps will not smell, and that they will burn brightly, and not expire suddenly because they have not been properly filled in the morning.

If the nursery is a small room I should advise the table to be made on the principle of one of the old oak gate tables in deal, stained a good dark brown. This is quite large enough to 'dine' four people, and can be used to cut out on, if required; and then when not in use it can be folded back and put against the wall, thus giving the child or children more room to play about. This table, a low chair or two, the children's chairs, and about two or three rush-seated chairs are quite sufficient furniture for a nursery, if we add a big cupboard which, if we are lucky enough to have recesses each side of the fireplace, can easily be constructed by any working carpenter. If there are no recesses I should put this cupboard in one of the corners of the room; it would take up less space there, and would not cause as many accidents as if it stood out into the room, always ready to deal blows to the unsteady toddler for whose sake such danger must be steadily avoided. The lower part of the cupboard can be sacred to toys, the higher part to work and garments in course of construction. All clothes in wear should be placed in a cupboard in the dressing-room, which room should also contain the nursery cups and saucers and property generally, and all washing and dressing matters.

An excellent thing for the nursery is a wide box-ottoman placed in the window, and if we can have one with sides and ends so much the better, as this can be turned with the back to the room, and here in a species of crib or cage, can a young person be placed safely to look out of the window, any attempts at falling over the back being frustrated by the nearness of the nurse. Of course baby cannot fall out of the window if open, or through it if shut, because of the most necessary nursery bars, which must be erected *inside* the window, not outside in the ordinary way; in this position they do double duty, and not only prevent accidents, from the child falling out of the window, but render it almost impossible for the glass to be broken. Of course a nursery window should be of plate glass if no other window in the house is, and should have a cheerful outlook, an amusing outlook being better for a child than any amount of toys. The window should be absolutely draught-proof. It must have a ventilator capable of being almost hermetically sealed in its top pane, and at the same time very easily opened. It must never be stuffed up with blinds and an undue amount of curtain. Sunshine means health, and the more sunshine a house or room receives the better. This should be impressed on a nurse at once, and she should never have the means of making the room dark and dismal in her hands, or else she will certainly do so at the very earliest possible opportunity.

Another most excellent thing to have in a nursery where there are growing children would be a regular hammock on good supports, to be erected or taken away at will, and to be sufficiently low to ensure that a fall therefrom would do no harm. This hammock would be as useful as a sofa, and as amusing as a swing, without the disagreeable after-effects and danger; and, of course, it should be heaped with the humble pillows, made of curled paper, in linen cases, which are so invaluable, because they cost nothing, and can be thrown about genially without doing any amount of damage at all.

The walls of the nursery must either be pictureless or embellished by really good autotypes, sufficient of which can be procured for about £5 for quite a large room. For let nothing allow any mother to put up the glaring vulgar nursery pictures which one sees so often in children's rooms, and which undoubtedly vitiate the children's tastes, and give them bad and false ideas of art from their earliest days. Then, too, I most thoroughly recommend that the amount of toys allowed be of the smallest: a Noah's ark, a really good box of bricks, a horse and cart, dolls, and a nice doll's house are quite sufficient for any small person. The child who is dependent on a constant supply of mechanical and expensive toys is a poor thing, and is never likely to grow up to be much good to itself or to anyone else.

If we arrange our nursery on these lines, and have the dressing-room also, we should require the simple bed for the nurse only to be brought into the room for use at night, and the dressing-room should be entirely kept for dressing purposes.

Our nursery needs a good cupboard. Wallace sells a good deal 'linen cupboard,' which, painted 'real ivory,' or electric turquoise enamel, makes a capital nursery wardrobe, and here the child's clothes should be kept, while the nurse should have one of Wallace's indispensable corner wardrobes for her dresses, which costs by the way the ridiculous sum of 28s. All that is required besides is a combination piece of furniture with drawers—toilet-table and washing-stand combined—and which would give her ample space for all the linen she possesses. One of Shoolbred's small bamboo cupboard-tables would hold boots and shoes and bonnets quite well, and no accumulations of any kind should be allowed. The nurse's box must never be kept in either room, but be relegated at once to the box-room; and directly a child's garment is outgrown, or the worse for wear, let it be given away. The only good I have ever been able to see in a small house is, that no one can possibly hoard there. If hoarding is begun it cannot be carried on, because if it were, there would speedily be no room to turn round.

Now, if one room only can be given up for a nursery, it must have fitments which can be removable at will in case we stay there not longer than the ordinary three years; or they can be on the lines of a 'workers' room,' I designed for Messrs Wallace & Co., and which said fitments are part and parcel of the chamber. In the first place the bed must fold up by day into a species of 'combined bedstead and bookcase arrangement,' which is a bed by night, and looks like a bookcase-sideboard by day; and in the second, another cupboard must be furnished with a shelf to draw out from above, resting on brackets: on which shelf are to stand the basin ewer, etc., when in use. The brushes and combs must be shut away, while the looking-glass should be an ornamental one over the mantelpiece.

With a room such as this the nurse must take the child to its mother when she herself is dressed, and she must throw up the window and open the door while she breakfasts with the other maid or maids. She must then 'do' her nursery thoroughly, and after that wash and dress the infant. While the child is quite small this should not be done later than 9 a.m; after it is a year old it must be dressed before breakfast, and go to its mother while the nurse has her meal. Indeed, no meals must be allowed in the nursery under these circumstances; and the fact of there being only one nurse means that the mother must act as upper nurse herself.

Such a situation I cannot recommend to any girl who has had but little acquaintance with the ways and manners of an infant. If she undertakes it, she will always be sending for a doctor; and, much as I love the profession, I would rather recommend the payment of a good nurse, for, if she is good, she knows far more about a baby than any doctor can do. He has most excellent theories, she a great amount of experience to aid her in wrestling with infantile complaints, which are generally treated far more satisfactorily by strict attention to diet, exercise and air, than by any amount of the newest and most wonderful drugs in the world.

If there are a couple of deep recesses, one each side of the fireplace, it would be quite possible to treat the room on the principles of the worker's room and at no great expense. In one recess should be a folding bed, closed up in a cupboard during the day time, exactly on the same lines as the Harrow boys' beds, and into this cupboard all the bedding can be shut. The second recess should have four or five shelves fitted in, and these should be covered by doors in three divisions. The upper and lower doors should be shorter than the centre one, and they should all shut and open quite independently of each other. The top cupboard should be used for garments; the second one should enclose two shelves, the lower one of which should be double width and hinged half way, so that when in use, it could open out and be brought forward and be supported on folding brackets. This shelf must be painted with Aspinall's bath enamel or else covered with white American leather to resist the action of water; and on this the washing apparatus must be arranged. Above, on the first shelf, all brushes and combs may be placed, while the glass over the mantelpiece can be used as a dressing-glass, or we can have one fixed inside the cupboard door that faces the light. On the other door should be fixed a brass rod for towels, then all would be complete. The cupboard under this shelf could be used on one side for the slop-pail, etc., and on the other for boots and shoes. These fitments could be made out of deal by any decent amateur carpenter. The wood could either be 'goehring,' which cannot warp or crack, or else well-seasoned deal, 'primed for painting.' It should receive a coat of Aspinall's enamel, and after two days have elapsed and allowed that coat to harden thoroughly, a second should be applied. Paint is saved and a good decorative effect is obtained by filling in the panels with Japanese leather paper or else with anaglypta, while carved panels can be bought very cheaply in the material 'goehring,' which of course would require the same amount of paint as would the rest of the cupboard fitments. Then the window-seat can either be the box-ottoman one already suggested, sold by Story & Triggs for about £6, 6s., and called the 'Desideratum,' or it can be made at home from more deal or more 'goehring.' In this case the simplest way to proceed is to put a straight piece of wood right across the bow or Caldecott window, hiding it by a flounce of cretonne. The back of the window would form the back of the ottoman, while the bottom could be made of brown holland, tacked in on the inside all round. The hinges of the top should be fixed to the back of the window, and the sides should rest on wooden bars nailed on the sides of the window, and the top should be composed of a stout deal frame, supplemented by straps of webbing, and on these straps a cushion should be laid stuffed with flock. This box should be made very strongly indeed and need cost very little; but although it holds a great deal, and can be most useful to supplement the cupboards, it can never be half as serviceable as the real box-ottoman with the ends and sides of which I have already spoken.

The decoration of such a room as this must depend on the aspect. If this be very sunny, as indeed it should be, green or blue should be used, the latter for choice. I do not think anyone who has not tried it can have the smallest idea how delightful this colour is to live with, or the use of it would be far more universal than it is even now. Of course people get the wrong blue, and then rave against it, and rightly too, for a drab or dull shade is simply awful. There are some shades which go black or grey at night, but no difficulty is found where Aspinall's 'electric turquoise' or 'hedge sparrow egg' blue is taken as one's guiding star. An *old* turquoise, or a rather dark-coloured duck's egg are also very useful as guides to colour, should Aspinall be unprocurable, and the rather prohibitive price (4s. 6d. a piece) puts Smee's Panton blue paper entirely out of the market, as far as a small suburban nursery is concerned. The cupboards and all the paint can also be of a soft brown shade, and then the dado should either be in anaglypta painted the same colour, or else in a blue and brown cretonne, which can be found sometimes at Colbourne's, or at Liberty's or at Oetzmann's. Above that should be hung one of Knowles's less expensive blue papers, if one can get it the right shade and he generally keeps it now, or the ever-faithful blue 'Olive-leaf' on which we cannot improve for a small room. The furniture should be as advised before, though, if the room be tiny, and there is only one child, Derry & Toms' folding-table at 4s. 11d. is quite large enough for all purposes, and leaves us far more space in the centre of the room than we should otherwise possess.

If the room is sunless: well, I should like to say that this is impossible: but, alas! I know that it is not: the room should be done in yellows and browns, and have blue curtains and carpet. But a sunless room is a crime, and should never be allowed. Neither should a tree-shaded house be chosen. Trees mean damp and flies and all sorts of misery; and if the trees which luxuriate in some suburbs cannot be cut down these suburbs must be avoided, for trees are all very well in their way, and lovely and pleasant enough in a big park, but they always come much too close to a small house, and I personally have been almost crippled with rheumatism and obliged to make two or three expensive moves, because I did not understand how very much the nearness of trees to a house had to do with the damp which caused me so much unnecessary suffering. Besides they keep out sunshine and light, and moreover harbour insects and dirt; and I think flies are among those miseries of suburban or country life which are never properly taken into account when folks think and speak of the delights of either existence.

By the way talking of flies let me give one or two simple ways of dealing with these torments and with their friends, the wasps, which however should never be destroyed heedlessly, because they in their turn prey on the flies and reduce their numbers pretty considerably. For flies the eucalyptus spray is a capital treatment, the only drawback being the extreme stickiness of the eucalyptus water which falls about, and often marks our cherished possessions. Then, Sanitas is very valuable, and if people are not sensitive to smells, no flies have ever been found which would face carbolic acid, a fact that I proved during one damp summer, when we were almost eaten alive by the little wretches. For one of my children caught scarlet fever, and the moment the orthodox sheets were erected, and the mop used freely on the floors to spread about the same disgusting stuff, with one accord the flies departed, and as far as I can make out have not yet returned at anyrate in any great numbers. I discovered, too, that wasps dislike eucalyptus, but not as much as flies do (these by the way retreat also before paraffin), while they vanished absolutely before Liberty's 'joss sticks.' These when burned liberally, kept them entirely at bay, and that in a year when the newspapers were filled with complaints as to their numbers and ferocity. Gnats are sometimes circumvented by hanging 'southernwood' on the bed, or about the windows, while, if the house be old or much covered with creepers—I advise nothing but tiny virginian creepers and clematis, roses bring blight and increase one's insect troubles at once—it is absolutely necessary to stretch very fine black gauze or net on a frame to cover entirely the window outside. This keeps out every insect, does not show, and does not keep out the very smallest amount of air or light. Only are earwigs circumvented by these means, or by a liberal use of disinfectants and of paraffin, but such remedies are to me worse than the disease and can only be employed if folks are not highly sensitive to smells. Carbolic makes me physically sick for hours at a time, and I think even the worst plague of flies which was ever experienced is better than the misery and discomfort of almost perpetual nausea. But when carbolic has not this effect it should undoubtedly be largely used to keep all insects at bay.

Now let us just for one moment describe a suburban house where decent nurseries are possible, where a good spare room is left, and a bedroom and dressing-room do exist, and which yet costs no more than £95 a year, for I see no reason why all small suburban houses should not be built on these lines. The staircase comes up from the hall to a narrow landing; on the left hand is the spare-room door, opposite that are good bed and dressing-rooms; and then on the right is an arch, beyond which are bathroom, day and night nurseries and a nursery pantry, designed first as a dressing-room to the room used for the night nursery.

This arrangement is small but perfect, for if infectious disease entered the nurseries, they could be isolated in one moment by a match boarding doorway erected in the arch and protected each side by the usual carbolic sheets. The strength of the carbolic, by the way, is 1 in 20, and the sheets are kept damp with an ordinary garden syringe. At the first hint of infection the rooms should be cleared of all superfluous furniture and draperies, and the carpets taken away and cleaned at once, while all floors should be mopped at least twice a day with the same carbolic as used for the sheets, etc., and in this every article used in the sick-room must be steeped before it leaves the place. Every mother and every nurse should know what to do on an emergency, and the moment anything infectious appears, the utmost precautions must be taken to prevent a spread of the complaint. Of course the doctor and the master of the house notify the complaint at once to the authorities, but the neighbours on each side and in front and back should be told too, and the tradesmen be warned; indeed, no precautions are too great to ensure that no one shall suffer by our fault or our carelessness and selfishness. Remember that we may be unconscious murderers if we are not super-careful at such times, for some child may die because we have not sufficiently realised the situation, or known how really wrong it is to run the very tiniest risk of giving someone else anything that may be fatal. As children more especially are liable to take infectious diseases the nurseries cannot be too lightly furnished, though of course, comfort must not in any way be neglected, nor must draughts be allowed. All curtains and *portières* must be washed, and the carpet and all furniture be removed at once, even if it have to be stored in the passages and other rooms, and be greatly in the way of the other inhabitants of the house. If the children have pets the dogs and cats must be washed with carbolic soap and water, and sent away at once, and the canaries must be removed downstairs. I do not think anyone realises how easily cats and dogs can spread complaints, else I should not have heard my nurse exclaim, 'Oh! I should never have thought of sending away the dogs.' Neither, by the same token, would the doctor, although both our dogs were in the habit of reposing on the beds, and one at least had extremely long hair.

To sum up briefly the necessities of a healthy nursery, I should say that they include two easily-isolated rooms, plenty of sun and air as opposed to heat and draughts, and above all, spotless cleanliness and well-made, simply-designed furniture, which can be easily moved, which allows of no accumulations, and which finally can be kept by the nurse herself in a state of perfect dustlessness without an undue amount of labour. Under these circumstances even a suburban house can be made to do its duty and to provide the proper accommodation for our future citizens the children of the home.

CHAPTER VIII

BEDROOMS

IN the rooms set aside for the purposes of rest and sleep, I venture to remark that the ordinary builder, to say nothing of the ordinary decorator, rises to his very worst heights of villainy, and makes the task before us one of almost superhuman effort. I have had three of these houses to live in, and in all of them, when the doors did not face the only possible place to put the bed, they came exactly at the side of the fire, and left no space whatever to put a sofa, let alone a comfortable armchair should one be ill and have to remain in one's room longer than the hours which are set apart for repose. And as illness is always possible, and moreover more than possible is it vain to ask when further 'eligible sites' are cut up for building, that the landlords of the future will kindly keep an eye on the

BEDROOM.

plans and ensure the houses being built in such a way that it is possible to live in them without an undue expenditure of money or resources? How I should love to design just for once the small ideal house with its square hall, capable of being used as an extra sitting-room or a billiard-room, we need not then have the 'three reception-rooms' which sound so grand and mean so little. Upstairs should be three good bedrooms and a dressing-room, bath and day nursery; the servants' rooms and box-room in their turn above these, and whenever possible, reached by a separate staircase. I see no reason why such a house with reasonable and rational servants' downstairs accommodation, as already described, should be out of the reach of the usual suburban resident with his £800 to £1000 a year.

If arranged in this compact and comfortable style, and if every labour-saving appliance that is obtainable is introduced, the number of servants required would be minimised. A great consideration in these days, when though we are always being badgered to help the unemployed no one seems able to get any servants, and, even if they are forthcoming, they have to be paid double the old prices, while they do half the amount of work. At least that is what I am always hearing. Personally, I have never found any difficulty in obtaining all the maids I myself require.

At the same time, if I were building ever so small a house, I should undoubtedly have hot and cold water taps and a waste pipe in every bedroom and dressing-room, and would even go as far as to have fixed washing-stands there too. I would put at least one cupboard in each room, also a window-seat, and, of course, the regulation tiled hearth and slow-combustion stove with its tiled surround and its simple black fender. The short curtains to the windows, the carefully-selected pictures and ornaments, and the matted floor should all help to make the work light, and to render it unnecessary to keep any superfluous number of maids.

But we have at present to do with the suburban residence as it is and not as it might be, and therefore it is not much use in dreaming about perfection, for if we do we shall most certainly be disappointed, and do no real good at all. We shall have to combat shrunken doors and ill-fitting windows, poor grates and bad floors, and therefore the sooner we set about remedying these faults the better it will be for us. I do most certainly advise that whatever else is put up with, the usual black wide-mouthed all-devouring grate may be altered and replaced with some kind of a very simple slow-combustion one. These grates can be bought for £3 or £4 at Shuffery's in Welbeck Street, and will probably save their cost in coal in one month's use. Besides which they will ensure the warmth and comfort which cannot possibly exist without them; for pile on coal as we may on the grate of the past, the heat goes mostly up the chimney, while the fuel is exactly as useful as regards keeping the fire in, as would be leaves or pieces of paper. Our sole occupation with such a grate is to jump up every five minutes and prevent the fire from going out altogether, by putting on more coal, and yet again more; until our patience, to say nothing of our coal supply, gives out most completely. I have recently spent some months in the company of such a grate, and I can assure my readers I have not had a pleasant time of it. I happened to be obliged to have a fire in all night, and I had no sooner gone comfortably to sleep than the cold roused me again to find that the wretched thing had gone out or almost out, notwithstanding that half an hour before I had not only fed it copiously with coal, but put briquettes in considerable numbers into its vast and hungry jaws. Briquettes which will as a rule keep in the fire for nearly twelve hours were useless here, and I have been therefore confirmed in my deadly hatred against these grates by my sufferings at their hands during a long and most exceptionally severe winter.

Once more, I can assure my readers as regards the grates, that it is absolutely no use to temporise; and that both the one in the day nursery and that in the best bedroom must go, even if it cannot be managed that the grates in the other upstairs rooms can be changed; while let nothing persuade anyone to have gas stoves erected. They are both cheerless and unhealthy, albeit I know they are a great saving in trouble, that they are now properly ventilated, and that they can be turned on and off at a moment's notice, and can be so regulated that the proper temperature for all rooms—60 degrees—can be maintained either at night or day. But I cannot breathe in any house where gas is allowed to warm the air. I know plants never last in such an atmosphere, as my plants do, and that, moreover, wherever gas stoves are employed largely, anyone in that special place is pale, wan and susceptible to cold. Indeed, the more I see of any attempt to heat our rooms otherwise than by open fires, the more I am convinced that such attempts are harmful and unsuccessful, and that, therefore, coal and wood fires should be 'our only wear,' at least until some genius invents something better and less costly. At the same time I don't see why anyone need make such attempts—given the proper grates—for nothing can take the place of a cheery blaze, which apart from its health-giving properties, always seems to greet us when we enter the room, is a delightful companion, and oftentimes provides us with a pleasant occupation should we be bored or tired. For nothing is more pleasing than to feed a good-tempered blaze until it laughs and chuckles at us as it goes rollicking up the chimney on its way to the outer air.

Then the last thing at night it can be banked up and left, rather dull-looking perhaps and surly and sad; but when the early morning comes one poke of the judiciously-applied poker and out leaps the eager blaze; a few good knobs of coal are put on, and in less than five minutes back comes our cheery friend, making even a foggy morning bright and cheerful, and a wet or snowy one vivacious if nothing else, under its bright and charming influence. What stove, what emotionless gas glitter can be anything save prosaic in comparison? while I am certain health suffers where anything save a proper fire is ordinarily employed.

A careful tenant can keep the landlord's grates and replace them when he leaves, but I never think this is worth the expense, the principal expense about changing the grates being the fixing them; at the same time, I cannot say too often that we shall not want to move in the insensate manner in which suburban residents do move nowadays, if we make ourselves comfortable at first, and do not sit down to discomfort, with that depressing sentence on our lips—'After all, it's only for three years, and therefore it is not worth while!'

Having begun our reform by putting in new and decent grates, we can turn our attention to the doors and windows and the floor. The draughts must be excluded by 'Slater's patent,' and the floor properly stopped, and moreover planed if rough; while should the door show gaps, as I once knew one to do, in a manner which allowed the unfortunate owner to perceive, without opening it, whether the gas was burning in the hall outside or not, these gaps must be stopped, either by inserting slips of wood, or with putty, or some sort of stopping: the door, as usual, being covered inside and out by the ever-useful, ever-faithful and most decorative *portière*. I cannot understand the firm and pugnacious way in which the ordinary householder clings to his bare and undraped doors, and will not avail himself of the shelter and warmth which can be obtained in no other way. It cannot be the expense. Wallace supplies the rods at 4½d. a foot, the brackets cost about 4½d. each, and as a yard and a quarter of double-width material suffices for the ordinary suburban door, though I advise an extra half width; and this costs, at the outside, 5s.; I see no reason why this should not be put over even the humblest suburban door in the world. As it cannot be the cost, I can but come to the conclusion that as usual paterfamilias has interfered, a thing no man should do in a house on the matter of decoration and management. He may give an opinion if he is asked for one: though he is most judicious who takes care that that opinion coincides with that of his wife, so if he has been hardy enough to veto the *portière*, he must be gently, but firmly, shown that it is not stuffy—the thermometer will do that—and that neither is it a dust-trap. This can be demonstrated in a few minutes by taking it down before his eyes, and having it removed, shaken, and replaced all in less time than it takes to tell of it. If after this he objects to moving it on one side as he enters the door, he must be carefully trained to see how ridiculous such a notion is, the while it is casually mentioned that an entrance to a room is not to be effected in the same way one takes a five-barred gate. This is a lesson all men can be taught just as many of them have been taught, thanks to me, that the hall need not be strewed with hats, gloves and brushes, and hung with coats and waterproofs in the last stages of dissolution, and that they can be quite as happy with their raiment out of sight as ever they were when they were allowed to strew it about in their entrances, at their own sweet wills. It is, however, usually impossible to live in an ordinary suburban house unless the furniture be made, in a measure for that special abode. For the rooms are so awkward and tiny that 'combination' furniture must be employed, or else one cannot have space to move.

No bed should ever be draped in any way. If the bedroom is properly arranged and ventilated, while all draughts are excluded, curtains cannot be required, and no bed need present a starved or undecorated appearance if pictures are properly arranged behind it, or a bookcase hung on the wall above it, and the pillows properly put into frilled cases, and placed during the day high up on under pillows. At night the look of the bed behind the sleepers cannot trouble them, but it will be all right if, as I said before, pictures are hung properly, just, and only just above the top rail of the plain and simple brass bed, the only kind which should ever be allowed in any house. If brass is too dear, then plain iron must replace it; the iron can be Aspinalled 'real ivory,' and so be made to look quite superior in every way, should the plain black iron be objected to.

I am quite shocked to see that a strenuous effort is being made to revive the beautiful, but unhealthy, wooden bedsteads of our ancestors, but I do hope someone will form an 'anti-wooden bed league,' and scotch the thing in its very earliest days, for there are people who will buy anything if assured by an enterprising tradesman that it is the newest thing out, and that a similar article was sold to a member of the aristocracy during the last week or so. Now, the very idea of the newness should warn off any wary buyer, for a new thing cannot have been really tried and found successful, while anyone can be fairly sure that a thing which has been sold, and sold largely for ten or more years, must be a success in one way or the other.

Really it does seem a little late in the century to combat the vast disadvantages of wooden bedsteads! still, it must certainly be done, else once more shall we have to put up with them, to the great detriment of our health. Just think how impossible it would be to make a wooden bed absolutely safe should infectious disease seize the owner! Then too it encourages insects, and is open to all sorts of other objections which those who think can discover for themselves. Therefore stick to brass and iron and the excellent wire-woven mattresses, which only need supplementing with a really good hair mattress to make an ideal couch, particularly if we see the latter is turned every day, and moved from the head to the foot of the bed, to ensure an equal amount of wear.

The simpler the furniture in a bedroom, the better it will be for the owner thereof, and if she can visit Hewetson and have real old Chippendale toilet-tables and washing-stands and wardrobes she should certainly do so; if not she should buy new things made on similar lines, and these she can always find at Smee & Cobay's, while for good plain furniture in a less expensive make, Wallace is always available, and should certainly be consulted on this ever-fascinating subject.

But I am indeed thankful to have to note that the brief reign of brightly-enamelled and coloured bedroom furniture is now at an end, as dead as the peacock's feather and the Japanese fan, and the dreadful stuffed storks and chenille monkeys so dear to the heart of the would-be artistic woman. Enamel is most excellent and useful if we must have the plain deal furniture, which we used to have to buy grained and varnished, and of an awful sickly yellow brown that would have ruined any room. But in this case we must buy the furniture in the plain wood 'primed for painting,' and either ask the upholsterer to follow our directions implicitly, or else have it home in this state, and paint it ourselves or turn on the handy man, without whom no suburban residence can be made in the least degree habitable, unless we can afford reckless expenditure, in which case we should hardly take up our residence in a similar abode. If this style of furniture be gone in for, it should be recollected that there are only two shades of enamel which can be used in a would-be artistic house for this purpose, and those are 'electric turquoise' and 'real ivory.' Green pink and yellow are truly terrible, and cannot be excused. Plain brown stain is bearable but I do not advise it, while let no one attempt to use an amateur green stain on any account. It is a failure at once and makes any room abominable because of its pretentiousness, for as I have said before, the beautiful green stain made familiar to us by Liberty first, can only be obtained from a professional hand, an amateur cannot get it, try how he may to do so. Now there are about three ways of decorating a suburban bedroom, though of course the details as regards special papers and special furniture can be varied infinitely. At the same time no one should make the fatal mistake of treating such a house or such rooms either in the Moorish, Japanese or Old Empire style, or in any eccentric fashion at all. Neither way can be suitable for it. Indeed, I do not care for the jumble of styles made by having an eastern-looking hall, an Old English dining-room, a Queen Anne drawing-room and a Moorish landing, which is so inexpressively dear to the would-be artistic decorator, and I can but suggest that my readers will resist the temptation of similar eccentricities to the very utmost, contenting themselves with the simple furniture kept by my pet firms, and using this in connection with the papers and paint which are specially made and designed to go with the different styles. If a really good hand-made floral paper can be afforded, nothing can approach it for bedroom decoration; but the printed cheap imitations must not be looked at for one moment, for they cannot possibly be the success the others are. Where a floral bedroom fails to charm, it is always because the paper is just not quite right, because every detail has not been thought out and carried out to the very smallest item, or because a timid person has advised on the subject, or the advice has been given by someone who does not understand the subject. Now to obtain success, Jeffrey's papers or Knowles's or Haines's must be used, and here let me name some which are always in stock, and which can always be procured. First of all is Haines's 'ragged robin,' a French paper on a soft ground, which is perfect; then comes Jeffrey's clematis in different shades and combinations of colour, my pet one being the mauve and green I have already mentioned, while Knowles's 'rose' and dahlia papers are beautiful, as are Godfrey Giles's, and although the cost is awful we must not forget Mr Smee's magnificent 'Hamilton,' albeit that could only be used as a frieze, as it is something like 10s. or 12s. a piece. Having chosen the floral paper the dado should be either in cretonne which matches the paper exactly; or else a dado should be made like a deep flounce in some plain material. If we select the cretonne, it must be run round the room so that the pattern goes in a different way to that on the wall, and the window curtains must match precisely. But should we select what Godfrey Giles calls the 'Muriel' curtain dado, the curtains should be in plain linen and lace, as should the table-covers, mantel drapery, and any cushion covers we may have in the room. Unless we use Miss Goodban's new linen and flax curtains, draperies, etc.; these, of course, are much more expensive, but then they are ideal, and the bedspreads at any rate should not be forgotten, for they wash and wear better than any others I have ever come across.

Then too the ware should match the flowers employed in the decoration; and in all floral rooms, save where blue and yellow are employed together, the floor should have either one of Wallace's square green carpets—the only green carpets on which one can absolutely rely to be always correct and always the same—or else plain cream matting or the green 'Isis' matting should fit the room as the old-fashioned carpets used to, supplemented of course with a certain amount of rugs judiciously arranged, and not put down in straight lines each side of the bed or in front of the toilet-table and washing-stand and fireplace, as they are all too often arranged by those who do not understand the matter. The paint should always be the exact shade of the ground of these floral papers, and this generally shades from pale ivory to still paler *café-au-lait*. Not that I mean for one moment that the paint in one room should be anything save one even surface of colour, but that as a rule the shade of the ground of these papers differs one from the other, and that whatever shade is chosen for the ground, that and that only must be taken as a guide for the paint for the room itself. Further, all cornices must be coloured cream and all ceilings, save those just written of, should be papered in some pretty and inexpensive ceiling paper, which, as a rule, in 'floral rooms,' should be Jeffrey's 'tie' paper in pale green and white.

The best furniture for these rooms is Wallace's set of green-stained furniture with tiles to match the shade selected in the wall paper; that is to say if we select pink and green, the tiles should be absolutely plain pale pink in the palest shade of coral pink, and if we have yellow and green, the tiles should be yellow; while if plain dados and curtains are used, the colour for these should be green as should the carpets. These rules should apply to any combination of colour we may select, the only exception being if we should have blue and yellow. Then blue must be our foundation, so to speak, while the tiles must be yellow and patternless, and the furniture in some good dark wood, such as walnut or Chippendale mahogany, my pet wood of all the woods one can buy.

If we select real Chippendale furniture, we should not have a floral room, although it would be correct to have one of the strange and to me hideous Chinese papers Knowles sells, and which were, I believe, the only correct wall papers at that special date, and which should be used with chintz, not cretonne, curtains. But then it would be still more correct to paint and panel the walls, and that would be singularly out of place in a suburban bedroom; unless we fell upon one of Mr Ernest Newton's little houses, when we should probably find the panelling ready for us and have nothing to do but paint it. Still I never can bear a plain painted wall, or one that is colour-washed or plainly papered. Such a room can never look really furnished, and has a most depressing effect; and in consequence I always advise paper; for, after all one had better be comfortable than correct. If we were absolutely correct, by the way, and remorselessly turned our backs on all anachronisms, we should have bow windows with tiny panes, rush-strewn floors and all sorts of detestable things which have long since vanished along with the 'bad old times' which gave them birth. Therefore as we will not be severely correct, we should have either an ivory anaglypta dado, and above that a 'sea-green' paper from Knowles or Smee & Cobay: or we should have an anaglypta ceiling coloured real ivory, and all sea-green finishings-off, as suggested before. Also we can use a really beautiful old-world material called linen damask, which can be bought of Smee, and which is a washable imitation of the damasks used by our ancestors, only in really beautiful colours, and not in the crude and awful greens, blues and reds which were so dear to their hearts. If the bedroom is sunless this green idea must be most studiously avoided; and yellow must take its place, arranged either with a dado or frieze of the anaglypta, or else with nut-brown paint and a brown linen curtain dado and yellow printed damask curtains.

A dado is far more useful in a bedroom than a frieze, for it saves the base of the wall from the tender mercies of the housemaid, and allows the bed to be placed against the wall, which is by far the best position for any bed; for, placed with the head and one side against the wall, it cannot take up half the space it does when stuck out into the middle of the room, as so many beds all too often do. I would by the way, most strongly recommend the beds which are known as 'twin bedsteads,' and which allow two people occupying one room to sleep quite independently of each other's movements, and which are therefore most invaluable in every way. There is no greater misery than for a restless person to have to control his or her every movement for fear of disturbing a bedfellow, no greater misery than for a quiet sleeper to be aroused every moment by some impatient gesture from a restless one: and all drawbacks are removed by having these twin bedsteads, which make each individual sleeper comfortable, and which also are very simple and well devised without any undue amount of embellishments.

Beds, by the way, should always be thoroughly dusted once a week, the entire bedding being removed for that purpose; while twice or three times a year the ironwork should be taken apart and well washed with Sanitas or carbolic soap, not because there is any chance of strange visitors having taken up their abode there, but because in no other way can one ensure the spotless dustlessness, to coin a word, that makes a house as healthy as it should most undoubtedly be. The third manner of decorating a bedroom, and the least expensive, is to take some definite colour—such as blue, yellow or pink—and 'live up' to that, and that only in that special room, taking care to choose an inexpensive paper in the right shade, and not deviating from it in the smallest degree. For example, the blue should be 'electric turquoise,' and none other. Knowles has always inexpensive papers the right shade, and if we avoid the detestable 'feather' which is dreadful, we shall be all right. Then the paint should be 'electric turquoise.' We should have a yellow and white ceiling paper, and should have Wallace's blue 'lily' or 'iris' square carpet, taking care to have a woollen fringe round it and a stained surround; using as always, Jackson's invaluable varnish stains. If the room be light, we can use Burnett's Bolton sheeting in the same blue, with a 'turned-over' top of the new-patterned sheeting to harmonise; but if it is dark and sunless the curtains should be yellow, in a similar material, although nothing should induce anyone to have coloured muslin curtains should the windows require a second set. All muslin curtains should be white, or at most only a faint shade of cream, and muslin curtains should be in all windows; upstairs and down; edged with very-softly-falling frills; unless the windows are 'Caldecott' ones, and therefore only require the one short set of material ones, which can be easily drawn and undrawn as required. In the blue room I am very fond of ash furniture and this can be bought at Wallace's quite well, but avoid here as elsewhere the ordinary chests of drawers, or my pet abomination, a chest of drawers to be used as toilet-table too; neither, under any circumstances, must a toilet-table be placed in the window; neither must 'half blinds' be indulged in. These two things look more vulgar than I can say, and are to be studiously avoided by anyone who cares about the outside appearance of her house.

If yellow be fixed on, we can have a real orange damasque paper, and ivory or brown paint, green carpet, curtains and furniture, or we can have 'buttercup' yellow, with 'earth brown' paint, matting and rugs, or else a brown square 'Dunelm' carpet from Wallace, Liberty's brown and yellow Java cretonne, and walnut or mahogany furniture. Or yet again the paint can be real ivory, the carpet and curtains blue, and the furniture 'real ivory' too, in fact a little taste and common-sense will provide an artistic room for any furniture that my readers may already possess.

If pink is chosen, there is only one paper I can really recommend as to colour, and that is a very old one: Pither's bay tree: which could be used with ivory paint, a deep frieze of Knowles's 'rose-garland,' and cretonne curtains to match, and here without any doubt at all we should have a green carpet and Chippendale mahogany furniture. I am very often asked by young girls about to get married what they can be working for their future homes, and I always say, 'very little,' unless they have already made up their minds what furniture they are to have, and how their rooms are to be decorated; because if they have a large stock of pretty things, pretty in themselves, they may find themselves either unable to use them at all or obliged to do so in rooms in which they become frightful at once, because they are utterly out of place. A room cannot be a success unless every detail dovetails and harmonises, and where the bedspreads, cushions and toilet-covers live in harmony with their neighbours; the curtains, paper and paint. However it is always safe to choose certain papers, such as those I have mentioned, and to work bedspreads to match, while, if we select pink as our leading colour, or yellow or blue, the flax and linen cushions and covers I have spoken of as prepared for work or worked by Miss Goodban can always provide occupation. Neither must it be forgotten that initials must be embroidered on the house linen, and that sets of sheets and towels must be kept for each room, and duly embellished with monograms in appropriate shades of Duncan's excellent washing silks.

Where a house fails to be a real success, be sure it is because some detail has been forgotten, and under these circumstances let no one rest until it is remembered and carried out. And here I am sure, is a great opening for an artistic woman with a keen eye for effect—if only she could persuade some of our larger upholsterers to employ her—for such a woman is badly wanted to go round every newly-furnished house, and note down as she goes the small things which will invariably escape the best male eye in the world, and even the eye of the best decorator. She will, pocket-book in hand, note the differences in the paint, which always occur where Aspinall is not used, the bolt or knob forgotten there, the curtain placed in the wrong room, the *portière* that has been left out, and she will finally put the last touches which none but a woman can, and which in some mysterious manner turn a house into the home it can always be made by anyone who really and truly understands the science. But nothing must be passed over; no doubt it takes time and thought to obtain perfection, still both are to be had, ay, even in the shoddy villa of the suburbs. But there must be no temporising, no 'it doesn't matter, it's only for a short time.' Neither must draughty doors and windows be allowed to remain; if so, pneumonia will come to stay, chronic colds will be our portion, and we shall be miserable from the moment we enter the house until we pass out of it in search of another, where we shall only once more meet with a similar fate; for the 'move on, please!' of the policeman is not worse or more constant than the silent hint given by the suburban villa that it is not in any way a suitable place of residence for us and ours, if we have not really circumvented its idiosyncrasies and made the very best of an absolutely bad job. Remember too, the great help a screen is in every bedroom which is big enough to have one without over-crowding, that one can easily have too many pictures and ornaments which encourage dust and enrage the housemaid, and that even the soiled linen basket should be chosen carefully. In these happy days, cheap things are quite as prettily designed as expensive ones, and if we take our time, know our shops and our own minds, and set to work carefully, there is nothing to prevent us nowadays from having a quite perfect house, and that without any undue expenditure of money or time.

CHAPTER IX

DRESSING-ROOMS AND BATHROOMS

LUCKY indeed is that suburban householder who finds himself the proud possessor of one or more dressing-rooms beside the orthodox bathroom, which, thanks to the march of the ages, is now to be found in the quite small houses which are only meant for such a humble individual as the ordinary city clerk. As a rule, there will be a dressing-room leading out of the 'best' bedroom, and if this need not be used as described in the chapter on nurseries, it were well to contemplate it and consider carefully if it cannot serve the purpose of a small private retreat for the house-mistress, should the 'third room' have to be devoted to the maids, or to the master, or even to schoolroom purposes. For it is absolutely necessary that she should have such a retreat; and if the bathroom be available for the husband as indeed it should always be in a little house, where visitors are the exception and not the rule, there can be no reason why the dressing-room should not be so arranged that the wife could use it in the daytime, ay, and even see her more intimate friends there, if she cares to do so. I have twice had houses which have had fireless dressing-rooms, and these were, of course, very difficult to deal with, even when the rooms were used as dressing-rooms only, and I do not quite know what I should have done had I not had other rooms available for myself. Yet as both dressing-rooms were on the outside of the house, fire-places or stoves could have been placed there, and, of course, ought to have been erected at once. But the bathroom in each case was used for a dressing-room, and the hot water always kept at a proper state of warmth even in the coldest weather; though in both cases fire-places were available had it been necessary to have greater heat. But when frost appeared we were always ready for it; we kept gas and fires burning whenever pipes were likely to freeze, and as all the outside pipes were properly protected, I have never had a pipe burst myself and have never experienced in my own person the miseries I have had so graphically described to me by sufferers from this most disagreeable consequence of carelessness and the improper manner in which pipes are fixed and the supply pipes managed by the ordinary water company.

But first let us consider how the dressing-room can be arranged should it be necessary to use it during the day as a species of sitting-room or boudoir for the mistress of the house. Of course all dressing-rooms should be painted and decorated to match, or else to harmonise with the bedrooms to which they are attached, but I think a harmony rather than an exact copy should be the aim of whoever wishes to use this room as a boudoir for some hours at least during the day. Suppose, for example, we have a very sunny bedroom, and we have selected a soft green paper, such as Smee's 'green ash,' and a rose-frieze for it, in that case we could have a pale pink paper in the dressing-room above a matting, or Japanese leather dado in green and gold, with all real ivory paint, and the furniture here could be in the stained green wood which I always admire so much, and of which it seems impossible to tire. We could have the green 'Isis' matting and rugs on the floor, and the curtains could be of sage-green serge; this would make a charming room, and while it would not slavishly copy, neither would it flatly contradict the scheme of colour in the bedroom.

In the same way a blue bedroom could have a yellow dressing-room attached, and this could be managed by selecting some real yellow paper, and placing it above either a gold-and-brown Japanese leather dado, or, yet again, above a matting dado, remembering that the matting used for this purpose must never under any circumstances have the smallest pattern on it; if it have, the look of the wall will be spoiled and the decorations will be anything but a real success. I am compelled to impress this fact upon my readers, because I have often seen a house spoiled simply because a matting dado to the room meant to the owner merely a dado made of matting; and she had not realised that chessboard patterns or large diamonds are entirely out of place in this situation. The only matting that should be used is the thin plain string-coloured kind made on purpose, and which is sold at Shoolbred's, Oetzmann's, and sometimes at Wallace's for 10½d. a yard; sometimes Treloar sells it for something less in a roll of 42 yards, but this matting is essentially what the French call '*a vende d'occasion*,' and has often to be really looked for until the right thing is found. If by the way a red and cream paper is put above a matting dado, and red paint is required to be used, a matting should be found which has a red thread running through it in an irregular way; it must not on any account have a set or formal pattern on it, or it will not be the success that it deserves to be.

Yet another hint, on no account should the dado or frieze rail be in the least degree heavy, the lighter it is the better, and I do not care for it to be more than an inch, or at most an inch and a half in depth. A wider rail always brings itself far too prominently before us, and attracts undue attention, while the lighter the rail is the cheaper will it be; and once more I say use 'goehring,' and then matters will not fail to be all that they ought to be. If the paper is yellow and the dado is brown and yellow, the paint can be brown also, while the curtains can be blue, as can the carpet, or else plain, patternless matting can be used, and the usual rugs.

If a blue square carpet is preferred, and lucky is she whose house contains a dressing-room large enough for this, the 'Dunelm' carpet is the best to have. It is made in most excellent colourings, is all wool, and very thick, and, moreover, is very inexpensive considering its admirable qualities. But as a rule a dressing-room resembles a tube or part of a hall more than a room, and as such we must think about it. It is generally long and narrow, and has a window in the most awkward situation, with, maybe, the door opposite; while the fireplace, if fire-place there be, is about a foot to the left or right of the door, and admirably situated for anyone who may be on the look out for a cold. This absurd situation can often be successfully treated by making the door open into the room on the fire side, thus making the door itself act as a species of screen to whoever may be sitting in the room. This alteration gives at once a place for a box-ottoman or an arm-chair, or one of Hewetson's admirable 'courting settees,' which can be placed with one end against the wall, standing straight out into the room. The high back of this settee shields anyone using it from draughts, and these are further to be combated by hanging *portières* over the door, inside and out, which will complete the task, already satisfactorily commenced, by a judicious use of 'Slater's patent.'

Then we have to consider very seriously how to arrange for the raiment that all men collect in such astounding quantities, and from which it is so desperately hard to part them, try how one will to get possession of venerable garments, which are of no possible use to the owners, but which would be of immense service to many unfortunates who all too often have not only no decent clothes, but do not possess any at all. This is however a vice all men develop sooner or later, and as they are made absolutely miserable by casting from them the oldest rag they may have, it is best in extreme cases to let them have their foolish way, taking care the moth does not enter into possession, and at the same time ensuring that they have not over-much space in which to keep their miserly delights. In a 'combination' room all shirts and underclothes can be kept in a charming piece of furniture Liberty sells, and which looks like a cabinet mounted on a couple of good deep drawers. It is made in plain white wood, clamped and ornamented with beaten iron and is very inexpensive indeed. In the deep drawers can be kept shirts and trousers, while there are plenty of smaller drawers in the cabinet part for socks, ties, handkerchiefs and other garments; coats being kept in a second cabinet, or else in a box-ottoman, or hung up behind the curtains of Wallace's 'P. T. C.' wardrobe, which can be erected in any corner of the room and has nothing at all of the bedroom about its appearance.

I have seen a most admirable piece of furniture at Oetzmann's, which he calls a desk washing-stand, and which would really be invaluable for such a room as this. When closed it is exactly like a desk with a flat top, and could be used as such in the day time most conveniently, but the top must not be laden with odds-and-ends, books, paperboxes or similar encumbrances. These should all be in one of Shoolbred's capital little cupboard tables; another of these, by the way, being procured for the boots and shoes in wear. These cupboards would hold three or four pairs of each, as they have a division-shelf inside, and though I know starvation is suggested to the ordinary male, to whom such small provision of foot-gear is indeed nothing short of pauperism, I venture to suggest that it is sufficient for every day, and that the rest of the stock can live in a proper boot cupboard in some other locality, which can easily be found if the house-mistress is clever and able to see at once the utmost capacity of the special rooms which are available for such a purpose. Indeed, a properly-made boot-cupboard can stand on one side of quite a narrow passage, and would never be noticed; for it could be either the proper one Wallace makes on purpose for boots, or else be formed merely

by placing three narrow shelves, one above the other, the top shelf enamelled the colour of the paint in that special passage, and the whole concealed from view by a double serge curtain, nailed along the top shelf with ornamental nails. This curtain must not be run on a rod, for it is no trouble to lift it; while if it be on a rod, it will be always out of place, and leave the boots and shoes on view in the most embarrassing manner. The contents of the shelves can be kept from dust by nailing Holland on the shelves of a sufficient width to fold over the boots, and so keep them quite safely from any undue accumulation of dust, while the top of the outside shelf can be used for ornaments. But the fewer of these there are in any passage the better, especially in a small house; one does not require more dust traps than one is absolutely obliged to have lest the place should appear barren and devoid of prettiness and attractive plenishings.

The over-mantel must serve as a toilet-glass, and this arrangement I personally prefer to any other, especially in the winter; but if the husband shaves—as it seems to me so many more men do nowadays than formerly—despite the hateful influenza, fogs and other trifles born of the end of the century, a regular shaving-glass can be set for him when the room is put ready for him at night; this can be removed to the bathroom during the day and the room need not give it a home then on any pretext whatever!

It is an excellent thing to have instead of either the ottoman or the courting settee a sofa-bed which resembles a couch by day, and can be turned into a regular bed at night, for often such a bed can be most useful. I like the 'grasshopper' couch, which I have only seen at Hamilton's, at Ship Street in Brighton, but this has no provision for the bed-clothes. These could be placed quite well in a drawer made under the couch; or Shoolbred has a species of convertible box-ottoman which would perhaps be best, as the bed-clothes could be quite well placed there during the day. Yet another cheaper method would be to purchase one of the folding beds with wire mattresses complete, sold by Story & Triggs for about 18s. 6d. These could have the extra mattress and pillows put into frilled cretonne covers all day, the bed-clothes being folded and put under the mattress comfortably during the same period.

Of course, a deep cretonne flounce should be placed round the frame of the bed, which under these circumstances would look like an ordinary low broad sofa. The bed should be pushed against the wall, against which pillows and cushions should be placed, and this would make a species of back, against which it would be possible to lean most comfortably. Given this, the desk washing-stand, and two or three low and comfortable chairs, and I think little else is necessary.

If much sewing has to be done, a little work-table can always be brought here from any other larger room, for there are plenty to be had now which hold a great deal of work, and yet can be carried by one hand. I have seen one specially good table the top of which is deep and is fitted for all kinds of sewing, while the under tray has a bag-like top of sateen or tapestry drawn together by strings, and this, I am assured, is invaluable for holding socks and other garments which require mending and overhauling by materfamilias herself. I am no 'stitchist,' and I do not think I ever possessed a thimble since my very earliest schoolroom days, and even then it was more often lost than available for its purpose, and I can most certainly say that I never had the smallest desire to know how to sew, but there are heaps of women who love to work, and of course there are more still who are obliged to do it and take it as a matter of course. And if the special mistress who may want to use the dressing room during the day is in any way devoted to her needle, she must have a good work-basket which she can remove when not in use, and which can stand in the bedroom or sitting-room when she does not require it. If the dressing-room is thus arranged I am sure it will add immensely to her comfort, for here she will have a refuge from everyone, and be able to be alone for some hours during the day, in a room where she will not be easily accessible and which will have nothing of the bedroom about it. That, by the way, is a great consideration; for let no one, not even in the smallest house, fall into the desperate error of sitting in the room in which she sleeps. I have twice had similar rooms where, of course, the bedroom portion has been carefully screened or curtained off, but unless one is a chronic invalid, such an arrangement is no good at all, and even if one is ill, and yet is able to get up, it is far better to go into a second room on the same floor, for no screen or curtain can give one any sense of real seclusion, and no one can have a room properly aired or cleaned unless it is left when one rises and not entered, save perhaps for dressing purposes, for the rest of the day. Therefore resist the temptation of the idea of a combined bed and sitting-room, unless you are reduced to one room only for all purposes, or are not a householder, or are a 'paying guest' (polite language for 'lodger') in someone else's abode. Under these circumstances, Wallace's 'worker's room' must be sought after and found, and its arrangements of course, make any room habitable at once. If the dressing-room is used, as suggested, for a retreat, the bathroom must be arranged in such a way that the master of the house can dress there with comfort; but no garments of any sort must be kept there, neither must the linen closet be on any account near the hot-water apparatus which dominates the bathroom. If it is, the linen will become yellow and rotten, and in a small house it is much better to apportion the linen into so many special amounts for each room, and keep these portions in the rooms for which they are intended. An extra cupboard being put up somewhere: perhaps in the maids' sitting-room, in which all table-linen can be kept. Great attention must be paid to the linen closet, and something should be bought for it every year without fail. As a rule I am no friend to 'sales,' and believe not one jot in the 'ruinous sacrifices' and 'vast reductions' which characterise them, but linen can often be purchased most wonderfully reduced in price at such times, more especially at Walpole Brothers in New Bond Street, and the house-mistress should always avail herself of these opportunities to keep up her stock, not laying in vast quantities, but keeping it up to its full strength. Unless this is done it is wonderful how soon a small stock of linen wears out and disappears, and one has the vexatious and expensive task of renewing the whole at once, which no one should ever be called upon for one moment to do.

So many people possess what is called a 'hot closet' in or near the bathroom, that these words of advice are not so out of place as they appear to be at first sight when writing about this special chamber; but the charms of this said 'hot closet' must be resisted if the linen is meant to wear, while great care must be taken to see that every single thing sent home from the laundress is properly aired, not only before it is put away, but also before it is taken into use. Damp clothes may kill or maim a person for life, and clothes may quite well become damp again after the first airing, more especially if they are kept in the ordinary cupboard of the very ordinary suburban residence.

Now if the bathroom should have to be used as a dressing-room, it must not have more furniture in it on that account than would be placed there under ordinary circumstances, but it should be papered with a really good tiled and varnished paper, and the wood-work should be enamelled 'real ivory.' I think Godfrey Giles's 'Mexican Tile' paper simply perfect, but this is a little expensive; still, if it cannot be afforded, it will serve as a hint to go upon, and Mr Giles must be asked for something in the same admirable colouring, but in a less expensive make. At the same time a cheap paper will not do in a bathroom; if we use one, the steam from the hot water will soon destroy it and make it flabby and untidy; and we shall either have the expense of re-papering or have to endure the sight of a torn and spoiled wall, which will make us unhappy every time we enter the place. The ceiling in the bathroom should always be colour washed the same pale cream colour which is used for the cornice, and the floor should be entirely covered with cork carpet. If the window is overlooked at all, it should be filled in with cathedral glass in leaded squares, or else should be stippled all over; we should then have serge curtains to draw easily over the glass, but we should never put muslin here: it rots at once, and is always flabby and disagreeable to look at and touch, and no decorative considerations should allow us to put it where it must be so singularly out of place.

In writing of the bedrooms, I quite forgot to urge upon my readers the fact that they should never under any circumstances allow themselves to be talked into buying the detestable regulation towel-horse, which is always in the way, and can never under any circumstances be necessary, while no skill can make it anything save an eyesore. Its place can usually be taken by putting a brass rod on very small brackets at each end of the ordinary washing-stand, or on the wall itself should the washing-stand be a round or a corner one, while a good brass rod must be put on the bathroom wall for the same purpose, sufficiently out from the wall so that the wet towels do not touch the paper. Moreover in well-regulated houses, the bath towels should be dried by the housemaid at the fire, and each person should bring his or her towels into the bathroom when he or she is about to use it, and take them away again when the bathing is finished, the brass rod being used merely to hang up the bath blankets, though they also must be duly dried by the fire, and not be laid down on the floor except the bath be in the process of being used.

These bath blankets can be purchased ready embroidered of Mrs Hanbury-Jephson, Towcester, and, like every other thing, should be bought to harmonise with the colours already used in the decorations of the room. If we have some good brass hooks on the door on which to hang the raiment we either take off or are about to put on, and have also one good strong kitchen or Windsor chair, and a proper lavatory glass with a shelf to hold brushes and combs, we shall not require any more furniture here, for remember steam and heat spoil anything in the way of good wood or manufacture; but I do plead very hard for a lavatory basin, with hot and cold water laid on and a self-emptying basin. It does not seem very much to ask for, but I wonder how often such a contrivance is to be found in the orthodox small house? Yet it is in just such a residence that these necessities should be found, for if hot and cold water be easily get-at-able, what an amount of servants' work is saved! No one minds washing his or her hands in the bathroom, while if there is no such convenience, the maids have continually to be placing hot water in the bedrooms and emptying basins, to say nothing of the fact that heavy jugs have to be lifted and replaced every time the bedroom washing-stand is used. This is a thing which is bad even for a strong servant and hurts a delicate woman in a serious way, therefore let us hope that lavatory basins will soon be found in all houses, small and big, and that the labour-making washing-stand may soon be numbered among the dead-and-gone mistakes of an ignorant past.

Another thing that no one seems able to rise above is the usual mahogany margin to any fixed bath, which always become disgracefully untidy, and makes the bathroom look squalid before it has scarcely been used. If the house belongs to the tenant, I should advise him ruthlessly to paint the mahogany with Aspinall's bath enamel, which does not mark with water; if he is only a tenant, the margin should be covered at once with the American leather which has a woolly back, cut out and fixed to the shape. If this is not done, the expensive process of French polishing will have to be resorted to when the house is left; besides there is the fact to consider that the margin will always be an eyesore, because of the manner in which people will either rest the soap on it or put one foot up on it, or even sit on it, while they are drying themselves after their bath.

We should likewise always have plain, unpainted deal shelves put up for the hot-water cans in the bathroom; and if, as is the unsavoury case in many bathrooms, there is a housemaid's sink there, the shelves should be put just over it, and should have gimlet holes in them for drainage; this will keep them from rotting, as no housemaid I ever met could be persuaded to dry a can before she put it down, and months of wet cans are guaranteed to spoil and rot the stoutest undrained shelf which I ever came across. Oh! if only every single person would know and learn each separate detail which goes to make up the perfect house and housekeeping, life would not be half as expensive, half as 'sketchy' and untidy as it now is in the vast majority of households, where people are content to jog along comfortably if things are just bearable, and where no preaching will, I fear, induce them to cultivate the twin talents of observation and regularity, which alone suffice to keep any house going in the way it most undoubtedly should go.

When the bathroom has been used it should be properly aired, and the moment it is quitted the housemaid should go in, throw up the window, top and bottom, and take away and dry the towels. If the weather is cold, the fire or gas must be kept going night and day to keep out the frost, and always the floor must be wiped over and the bath blankets hung up until they can be properly dried, then will the room remain nice much longer than it otherwise would. The mistress of the house herself must see that the bath is properly dried after use, and that the basin and housemaid's sink are duly cleaned and disinfected. For even soapy water decays and smells, and drains that are used for nothing else can be as offensive, even if they are more innocent than others, about which lurk absolute and imperative danger. It is well to cover all outlets for water with very fine hair or wire netting. I personally prefer hair, as that is much finer than anything else. Then there is no chance of any drain being stopped up as nothing save water can pass through it. The sink basket sold by most ironmongers is a very good possession, and acts in much the same way, but the netting does just as well, and should be nailed across the housemaid's sink about an inch above the bottom, and be erected just above the plug-hole in a lavatory basin, thus saving endless heartburnings, and endless sending for that fearsome creature, the regulation British plumber. There should be no *portière* inside the bathroom door, but most certainly there should be one outside. It prevents sudden surprises, and, furthermore, conceals the room from passers by, should the door be left open, as is all too often the case, by either a careless maid, or a yet more careless user of the room!

There is one more aspect of the suburban villa to consider, I am sorry to say, and that is the one where there is neither a bathroom nor a room which can be adapted for the purpose, and where all baths have to be taken in the different rooms themselves. In such a house as this there must be large squares of American leather ready for use, to be covered in their turn by bath blankets, on which the bath itself can be placed. These would be for use in the bedrooms, and then the dressing-rooms must be used as dressing-rooms, and will allow of no compromise or other use at all. In this case, I very strongly advise a high dado of plain brown patternless linoleum or oil-cloth, having the paint the exact shade of the dado, above which can be either a good blue or yellow sanitary or tiled paper, while the floor must be covered entirely with plain brown cork carpet, on which one or two rugs can be placed, the inevitable bath-blanket being put under the bath itself, and the rugs put out of harm's way for the time. These precautions will allow of the wondrous amount of splashing which invariably marks the progress of a man's bath, while the furniture for such a room should be regular dressing-room furniture, removed as far as possible from the spot sacred to the bath. A good housemaid will carefully look over the furniture when she 'does' the room, and will rub off at once any marks of soapy water she may come across. But such excellent and conscientious maids are few and far between, except in the 'highest circles,' and they don't inhabit Suburbia; therefore should every mistress cast an eye over every room once a day, and see for herself that the depredations of her husband, and all too often those of her visitors too, are carefully eliminated.

It used to be difficult, nay well nigh impossible, to buy really good and suitable dressing-room furniture, and I have had many a painful hunt after wardrobes which were not evidently meant for the raiment of females alone; but now all is altered; and should we be able to afford it, we can buy an admirable wardrobe at Wallace's which has a place for everything a man can possibly require, and this with a boot-cupboard, an ingenious combination toilet-table and washing-stand, a couple of chairs, and a comfortable basket chair, form the most perfect equipment a man can want, whether he reside in the suburbs or in any other part of the civilised globe. But he must have no room for unending hoarding, else will the heart of the house-mistress fail her by reason of the fearful amount of rubbish he will accumulate, and from which nothing will induce him to part!

CHAPTER X

THE GREAT SERVANT QUESTION

IN the chapter about the kitchen arrangements, the most burning question of the hour was just touched upon, and a few hints were thrown out as a species of guide to solve the knotty problem, which certainly is more acute in the suburbs than in any other place. First, because it is often found impossible to coax the best maids away from the wiles and entrancements of the town; and secondly, because the accommodation for them is often little short of disgraceful. Though for the matter of that, I have seen worse servants' rooms in big houses in grand localities in London than in any other, while the rooms set apart for them in flats would be ludicrous if they were not so pernicious, and did not so largely account for the unpopularity of what ought to be an almost ideal place of residence for a husband and wife, who have either settled their children in life, or have no children to settle or think about in any way.

We have described at length how we should circumvent the ordinary suburban kitchen, now for a while, let us think about the servants' bedrooms, which are often quite as difficult to manage, and are all too often much too few to be in any way comfortable or decent. Should the general number of four maids be kept, or should a fifth be required, it is almost impossible to make an arrangement that only allows of the work being done properly and in order. I have had a large, a very large, experience of servants in more ways than one, and I venture to remark that where they are a nuisance it is because, first of all, they have not been chosen with care and common sense; secondly, because no attempt is made to make them comfortable or cause them to feel part of the household; and thirdly, because what I may call 'composite maids' are engaged. That is to say that the cook is required to clear the breakfast and answer the bell in the morning, and do a certain amount of housework; while the parlour-maid has to help with the beds, and the nurse to do the washing as well as look after, dress and walk out with the children. Now I state boldly that such a division of labour can never be either necessary or successful, and if the dwellers in the suburbs will amalgamate the several duties of a servant in this way, they can never know the least peace, for no servant worth her wages or even her salt will take such a nondescript position unless under very exceptional circumstances. These may include places where the mistress has taken her maids from the first, and has carefully instructed and brought them up herself, or they may be personally greatly attached to her themselves, and value not only her kindness but the comfort and comfortable home she gives them. But these circumstances are as rare as they are satisfactory. Therefore unless these things are the case, let no one abuse the maids unmercifully because they will not one and all be maids of all work, but rather consider how best to arrange the day's routine, so that each shall stick to her task cheerfully, giving presently a helping hand to another out of real good-will, and not because she is imperatively requested to do so as a matter of course.

Unfortunately there are hundreds of women who can neither give good wages nor keep a sufficient number of maids; and these are the miserables who join their wails to those others who, more unhappy still, have not the slightest idea how to manage another woman, whose one idea is that a maid is a thing whose capacity for work is endless, who can never tire, never want to go out, and who, above all, can never be ill. Such a mistress treats her servant as he or she does a horse who has never been used to possess this quadruped, and seeing only that it is made to go, drives or rides it to death, because previous experience has been wanting to teach the driver or rider the amount of work which can be obtained without undue exertion and pressure. Now it is necessary to point out that, if a sufficient number of servants cannot be employed to do the work decently and in order, the work must be lessened in some way or another, by the mistress herself giving a helping hand, and not only directing it but doing some of it. She must be content to call a spade a spade, and not have any hankerings after 'agricultural implements.' A cook she may not possess, a good general servant is what she requires, while a housemaid who can wait at table replaces the house parlour-maid who never did and never could have a decent existence or be anything save a miserable sham! If a good general servant, who can cook is engaged, at once the way is made plain before all concerned. Such a woman cheerfully keeps her own kitchen, the hall staircase (if in a basement), and front steps in order, and has the dining-room under her charge. She will likewise clear out the breakfast and answer the front door up to twelve, but she must not be called a cook; if she is, she will cook, but she will not for one moment step out of her province to do anything else whatever.

In the same way must the housemaid be managed, for in such an establishment the parlour work can but be of the most meagre description, and if the mistress is house-proud, and really has desires after fine and careful living, she must keep silver, glass and china clean herself, and see herself to the laying of the cloth and all the thousand and one items which go to form the finer portions of housekeeping. An occupation which will no doubt trouble and disgust the woman who demands to 'live her own life' and 'develop her soul' at the expense of the comfort of the household which she has undertaken to guide when she became the wife of the bread-winner. I am not going to express an opinion on the merits of a career, bounded by the nursery on the one side and the kitchen on another, there will always be a difference of ideas on the subject; but I am going to say very forcibly, that when a woman marries she undertakes this special business; and should she regret it or allow the reins to slip out of her hands, she is 'obtaining money under false pretences,' and is undoubtedly neglecting the work she solemnly promised to perform. Therefore, all women who marry must be prepared to face the situation and to know that before they can 'live their own lives' and 'develop their souls' as mentioned before, they must see that their houses are in order and that their houses are homes in the widest sense of the word.

People are continually writing to me, and also to everyone else who gives advice on the special subjects of house management and decoration, about this servant question, and, moreover, as continually ask how to divide or apportion their special incomes to their special wants; but they cannot see how utterly impossible it is for a complete stranger to do more than vaguely generalise on either subject. The servant question has always been simplicity itself to me, and I cannot understand the difficulties which beset so many women in these days, simply because I have never come across them myself. But then, I do not expect perfection. I give fair wages, and am as considerate to the maids as they are to me, and I am not unduly dismayed or cast down when I discern faults and failings that are human after all, and denote that at present, at least, we have not reached the golden age. At the same time, I am convinced that the real trouble, as I said before, is caused in small houses by the 'composite maid' being called a cook, or house parlour-maid, when she is just either a general servant, or else a housemaid; and in larger ones by sufficient care not being taken to obtain the kind of maiden one really does want, and by expecting too much from her when she is in our service.

The life of the ordinary domestic servant, despite the delirious joy of the tradesman's daily calls, is an extremely dull one. The routine is everlasting, the relaxations few, and the changes still fewer. In many households a friend to tea is a crime; an unexpected holiday an impossibility; while the days follow each other in a wearisome routine which would tell on the nerves of anyone even far more highly educated than is the orthodox maid-servant. How many brilliant summer days pass, and no one suggests an afternoon or evening stroll, or even a drive through the country lanes. How many dreary winter days go by, and no one says there is a good play at such and such a theatre, go and see it. Or who takes concert seats, and sends off the maids for a couple of hours from the everlasting kitchen and the weary round of unending duties? Well, some people do, and where this occurs there the maids often stay on and on, giving real and loving service, and doing their utmost for those who try to do their utmost for them.

Then once more how few maids really have and possess their mistress's confidence. They hear a vast amount of grumbling about 'the books,' and the dreadful waste which does go on, often enough more through ignorance than through their carelessness; but they do not comprehend that there is an all-important reason why such waste should not be allowed, because the mistress has never explained matters to the maids, or told them there is necessity for great care in all the household departments. As a rule servants have what they consider the 'honour of the house' very near their hearts; and they cannot endure the notion that their mistress shall even be suspected of 'meanness.' And this is often the cause of the needless orders given in those establishments where the tradesmen are allowed to call; for, rather than send them away without an order, the servants will rack their brains to think of something, not because they really desire to swell the bills, but because they like their house to be one of which the tradespeople speak well, and because they will not have it spoken of as a 'mean sort of place, where every halfpenny is counted and made to do the duty of a penny piece.' Then too, at the bottom of a great deal of domestic mismanagement is the utter and really ghastly thriftlessness of the lower classes, which no one who has not seen it could credit.

I have had to be a great deal away from my own house, owing to long-continued illness, and in consequence I have seen a great deal of the way in which other people manage, and I boldly say that I have seen more waste and real extravagance among people who ought to save absolutely every bone and piece of bread than among those who could really afford to waste, did they not consider it wicked to do so. While the lower one goes in the social scale, the more one finds waste the order of the day; and not only actual waste, but the waste of having the best joints, the most expensive butter, and the continual variety of food that no one in the upper middle classes can afford, even should they think it necessary to have it. I have noticed real want existing among a specially improvident set of people, while, at the same time, I have been shocked to see great lumps of meat and bread (unpaid for) in the pigs' tub. The young people of these households would have their boots blacked for them, their hot water and bath water carried up for them, and be waited on, before they went out to their shops or work, as one's own children would never dream of being waited on, in a much much higher rank of life. In these households the servants have simply an awful time of it, and hence class prejudice is fostered terribly, while the unthrifty ways of the household leave their mark on all who pass through it, and help to build up a class that is in every way unsatisfactory.

We hear a great deal of the competition of the foreigner, and there are loud shouts for 'protection' and 'fair trade,' but the 'protection' we want is against our own wasteful habits and ways of living, and we can never have 'fair trade' until we comprehend what waste really is, and know what is necessary to keep a household going and what is not. And this servant question is the very *crux* of the whole matter, and, alas! is very little understood by the public at large, which seems quite incapable of grappling with the problem, although few people exist who have not a more or less loudly-expressed opinion on the subject.

It is also a problem which can never be solved until all have learned real thrift and carefulness, and until all classes learn how to trust each other, and the special conduct which should be maintained in all relations in life. Though the tendency nowadays to live in flats, and have as many meals as one can at a restaurant or hotel, may solve the servant question quicker than in any other way, regardless of the fact that a class of useful women will thus be improved off the face of the world in a manner I, for one, shall be extremely sorry to see. But flats are fleeting joys at best. I have heard of many people going to live in them, and have never known anyone renew his or her lease; so perhaps the pendulum may swing back again, and houses become the order of the day.

As long as servants are required, the best way to obtain them at first is for the young mistress to train them herself, always keeping on hand an under-study for the part of the upper-servant in the shape of kitchen and under-housemaids; in this way lie a sure success and comfortable domestic arrangements. Of course there are hundreds of small establishments where a couple of maids is all that can be allowed. These must be as described before, general and housemaid, then all will go rightly, providing care is taken to obtain good girls from good families, who have not been spoiled by a careless or bad mistress, or ruined by an unhappy and thriftless home training, which is often indeed worse than none. In a larger house where there are children; six maids and a boy to help, are the maximum; namely, cook and kitchen-maid, parlour-maid and housemaid, nurse and nursemaid; here again things will be all right, and there will be no over-work or under-work in the matter. Lucky is she who, by tie of birth or friendship, is connected with some country town or village, which shall act as her preserve, and from whence she can always draw fresh supplies should matrimony or other cause thin her domestic ranks and compel her to look out for another maiden.

But in all and every case should the registry office be most carefully avoided. If a servant or mistress has a 'good name,' exceptional indeed must be the circumstances that drive her to make use of these places. If a decent maid is leaving her place, the tradespeople know all about her and will tell her of the good places which may be open; and in the same way a really 'good place' doesn't go begging. The tradesmen know of that too, and often act as a sort of informal registry-office which I have invariably found most useful in every manner. Then having caught one's maids, let us consider how best to keep them, and undoubtedly is this done by making them as comfortable as we can, and by showing that we have a real interest in whatever they may have or do.

I have already written about the room they should have to sit in. Now let us consider those they should have for sleeping purposes, for often these are as badly arranged as they can be; economy is studied on the one hand, which on the other results in an amount of expenditure which is as unnecessary as it is worrying and distasteful to all concerned. One of these petty economies is that which consists of making a couple of maids share one bed, and that one anything but a comfortable place of rest and refuge. Now this should never be done. The economy consists in the saving of the washing of a pair of sheets, the misery comes in when the unwilling bedfellows quarrel and determine to move on elsewhere. In no case should more than two maids sleep in one room, and in every case such room should hold a couple of beds and a double set of washing-stands, drawers and toilet-table, and, moreover, there should be a good hanging wardrobe of some kind. If possible, once more the ever-useful P. T. C. from Wallace's should be pressed into the service, and should decorate a couple of the room corners, one being devoted to the use of each maid, whose dresses will last twice as long if she have proper room for them, and if she have not to cram them into her small chest of drawers, shared all too often by her fellow-servant.

I consider Knowles's sanitary papers quite ideal for the maids' bedrooms, and there is a dainty 'daffodil' paper that no one can dislike or despise, and which can be wiped over once a month, if necessary, with a damp duster and come out as clean as a new pin. With this paper we could have earth-brown paint, and Liberty's ever-useful dark blue and white butterfly cretonne, edged with frills, and blue and white dhurries on the stained floor. But if the floor is bad, and in the least degree draughty, it must first be covered with cork carpet, on which rugs or the ever useful dhurries can be laid down. Some suburban floors are amenable to no other treatment. We may plane them carefully, and 'stop' them as carefully too, but they will begin to gape at the smallest change in the weather, or at the sight of the first fire, and one can neither keep out the draughts nor the gently-drifting dust that penetrates at every corner, and spoils tempers and properties alike. Cork carpet I consider a most blessed invention, as it makes a capital background, and is warm and comfortable and quite spotlessly clean. This should be 'gone over' once a week in bedrooms of this class with a damp duster; and once a month should have a healthful polish with Jackson's camphorated beeswax polish, made on purpose. The rugs should be shaken out of doors once a week, and, whenever possible the beds and bedding should be alike exposed to the sun and air in the garden; or, if not, in the rooms themselves, taking care that all windows and doors are open and a thorough draught ensured.

Indeed if we got more sun and more air into all our houses, every girl's health would be far better than it is now; but despite all the preaching in the world, English women stuff up the windows with blinds and curtains, and shiver at the idea of fresh air, while they dread the fading of their curtains and carpets in a manner that would be ludicrous were it not so essentially harmful. Naturally too the genus domestic servant dreads open windows more than her mistress does, and will not air her bed if she can possibly avoid doing so. But if there is a rule that a fine, hot day shall see the mattresses, blankets and pillows on chairs in the garden for at least an hour after breakfast, the airing is ensured without the 'poking and prying about,' which is as distasteful to the mistress as it is disagreeable to the maid. In all cases too, the beds here as elsewhere, should consist of good hair mattresses laid on chain mattresses. These chains should be covered first by a square of holland, tied at the four corners, and this should be sent to the wash about every three months. The mattresses and pillows should be covered also, either with crash or holland cases, capable of being washed whenever necessary, and these covers will save the beds immensely from wear and tear, and ensure cleanliness at the same time. Wallace has a very good suite of servant's furniture to sell for something under £5, but I think we should spend rather more on the bed, which is a very fair one, but not quite good enough if we are very particular, as we should be, about the comfort of the bed, as a hair mattress is impossible for this sum, and a hair mattress must be had if the bed is to be a real place of rest. Furthermore, I think the beds should have two pillows, as well as a bolster, and a second pillow should therefore be added, and all beds should have five blankets: one for the under blanket, and two pairs for over use. These should be sent to the wash in the spring; one pair at a time; and the beds should be supplemented with good heavy coloured counterpanes; the colour looks cheerful, and also ensures the quilts not looking dirty before they ought to.

The simpler the sets of ware the better, for, somehow, china never lasts long in the ordinary servant's room. I think she rushes up at the last moment to wash and dress; she certainly gets up in the morning at the last possible instant she can, and the usual results of haste ensue. The handles come off the carelessly-seized jug, the soap-dish flies about, and the basins are literally 'whacked' down, because there is not time to treat them properly, therefore the excellent sets of blue and white ware Wallace sells at about 4s. 6d. should be the outside price to which we should go, taking care all the sets are alike; then one can supplement the other when smashes begin; and quite plain glasses and water-bottles should also be procured, in as stout a make as possible. Glass tumblers literally vanish in servants' bedrooms, and I am often amazed at the way in which they disappear, one after the other, to a grave on the ash-heap or in the dust-bin.

Another thing on which we may with advantage spend a little more money is the looking-glass, and that without unduly encouraging vanity, for the usual one sold with the cheap suits is much too small to be of any real use. A girl cannot do her hair and arrange her dress neatly unless she has a glass large enough to allow of her doing so by its aid, and we should therefore choose the maid's looking-glass as carefully as we should our own; but we should allow one each, if we wish for peace. More domestic quarrels are caused by the usual one small glass than many house mistresses are probably aware take place at all.

It is certain that all mistresses should, at least twice a year, thoroughly inspect all the furniture in the maids' rooms, and replace then if possible, all that has been worn out during the past six months, but under no circumstances should this inspection take place without the presence of the maids, or when it is not expected. Nothing is more disagreeable to the ordinary mind than the idea that one's room is not one's castle; and many mistresses have made themselves eternal enemies by insisting on their undoubted right to enter any room in their own houses whenever they wish to do so. That the right is so undoubted should render it unnecessary to exact its performance. By all means see the rooms are all right, but do it at a proper season, and without the smallest idea of 'pounce' in it.

I do not think it wise to have gas in the maids' rooms, unless it is turned off at the meter by the master at a certain hour, and yet it is undoubtedly safer than any other light, and is as undoubtedly cleaner. I have for years used nothing save the little 'Butterfly' lamps sold by A. & A. Drew, of Wareham, Dorset, but these are not good in careless hands, because the chimneys are so constantly being broken, and because the oil is capable of being spilled. Candles are worse possessions, as so many maids will read in bed, will smash the shades without which no candle can possibly be safe, and will drop grease from them on every available space. Remembering also that the dark winter mornings have to be considered, I am fain to retract my old belief that gas in a servant's room spelt ruin, and to allow it reluctantly, placed near the looking glasses and not near the beds, and having woven-wire globes to protect the flame, similar to those used in places of business and in large schools; as the ordinary glass globe has even a shorter existence than the tumbler, and is broken in less time than it takes to tell about it.

If in any way possible, the beds should be placed against the wall, and foot to foot, with about 2 feet space between the ends of the beds. In this case a dado should be run round that portion of the wall where the beds stand, and this should be of plain brown patternless oil-cloth, and should have a real dado rail; this would keep the wall tidy for years. In no case must the dressing-tables be placed in the window, and blinds must never be allowed. If there is much sun, the dark blue and white cretonne curtains can be lined with still darker blue sateen, and if the windows are large muslin can be stretched upon them as in all other windows in the house; but blinds are an expense and an abomination. They are always out of order, are very rarely drawn up straight, and are as needless as they are dear and unsatisfactory. The dark curtains draw easily and cannot be drawn crooked, and are in every way much more sensible and useful than blinds.

I think that there should be fireplaces in all servants' rooms. First because of the ventilation a chimney affords,—and the bi-annual inspection should include a glance at the chimney to see it is in nowise stuffed up—and secondly, because it is imperative that we should be able to have a fire there if necessary. It may sound improbable, but it is true, that the average suburban villa is colder than the cottages from which country maids come, where the thatched roofs and the thick walls often keep out extremes of temperature in a manner a jerry-built house ever can.

And here is one more hint. Let the roof of the house be white-washed in summer, if it be slated and the bedrooms come right up under it, for this makes an enormous difference to the temperature of the rooms, which is often enough simply awful even in a merely average summer without any very abnormal heat, while, should we have any real heat, these rooms become similar to ovens, and are really terrible for anyone to have to sleep in. Then have outside blinds of some kind; plain strips of dark green or blue linen placed outside the glass are better than nothing, though Williams' green reed blinds are the best things in the world, if they can be afforded; and above all white-wash your roofs. You will be rewarded in the difference in the maids' tempers, and health, which, are very often one and the same thing.

Now just one word more, and that on the vexed subject of food. You should feed the servants as much as possible as you feed yourselves, and then will you have peace and not otherwise. In another place I have dwelt at large on this matter; here it is sufficient to say that if a thing is good enough for the dining-room, it is good enough for the kitchen. Allowancing should never be resorted to, there is something about it that revolts the kitchen or servants' hall, and it is as unnecessary in a well-managed house as it is useless and suspicious.

It will be seen, from the perusal of this little book, that the art of living in a suburban house is not quite as easy as it appears at first sight. At the same time it is without doubt one that can be acquired, and if our lot should be cast in the suburbs, it is positively necessary that we should learn to live there comfortably, unless we wish to be always on the move. Should what I have written on the subject help anyone to circumvent the special house he or she has selected, and to turn it from an unsatisfactorily-built villa into a comfortable home, I shall not have written in vain. At all events, the book has one merit, it is the outcome of real experience, and there is not a single ounce of imagination in the whole of it!

THE END.